THE ROLE OF RELIGION IN ETHNIC SELF-IDENTITY

A Vietnamese Community

Paul Rutledge

UNIVERSITY
PRESS OF
AMERICA

LANHAM • NEW YORK • LONDON

Copyright © 1985 by

University Press of America,® Inc.

4720 Boston Way
Lanham, MD 20706

3 Henrietta Street
London WC2E 8LU England

Library of Congress Cataloging in Publication
Data

Rutledge, Paul, 1945-
  The Role of Religion in Ethnic Self-
Identity.

  Bibliography: p.
  1. Vietnamese Americans--Oklahoma--Oklahoma
City--Ethnic Identity. 2. Vietnamese Americans--
Oklahoma--Oklahoma City--Religion. 3. Vietnam--
Religion. 4. Oklahoma City (Okla.)--Foreign
Population. I. Title.
F704.041R87   1985   305.8'9592'076638   84-25781
ISBN 0-8191-4505-X (alk. paper)
ISBN 0-8191-4506-8 (pbk.: alk.paper)

DEDICATION

This book is respectfully dedicated to the Vietnamese people of Oklahoma City. It was their assistance, friendship, and cooperation which made this study possible.

ACKNOWLEDGEMENTS

I should like to express my sincere appreciation to John A. Dunn, Chair, Department of Anthropology, University of Oklahoma, for his personal encouragement and invaluable assistance in the formulation of this study. In addition, I should like to acknowledge the contributions of William Bittle, Donald Brown, Sidney Brown, and Stephen I. Thompson. Each of these persons in their own special way provided assistance and insight into the field work and research procedures.

In addition, I should like to express my appreciation to Huynh Sanh Thong, the editor of Vietnam Forum, Yale Southeast Asian Studies, both for the kindness in allowing me to use a previously published article (Vietnam Forum, Summer-Fall, 1983, no. 2) as the basis for Chapter Two, as well as, for his personal encouragement.

I should like to thank Wanda Downs for her assistance in the initial typing of the manuscript, as well as Tina Leone who assisted in the typing of the final draft and in the preparation of the manuscript for publication.

I should like to acknowledge with deepest appreciation my family--Suzanne, Jeremy, and Maile--whose love and encouragement has motivated me from the beginning.

TABLE OF CONTENTS

LIST OF FIGURES

Page

CHAPTER I

INTRODUCTION

"It was hard for me to get here.   It will be
for me to go back to my country. But someday
I will go back to my home again."

Vietnamese Refugee Man
Oklahoma City, 1981

The Vietnamese Entrance into the United States

With the evacuation of America troops from Saigon in 1975, one of the largest mass movements of people in modern history began. Many Vietnamese who had supported the United States presence in their homeland fled the approaching army from the North. Fearful of the Communist government (Liu, 1979), they left their homes and often portions of their family in order to seek refuge in other countries. In April 1975, "over 40,000 Vietnamese were evacuated by airplane and helicopter from Saigon, and an additional 67,000 Vietnamese escaped by boat into the South China Sea" (Brown, 1981:1).

The flight from South Vietnam resulted in a scattering of people throughout the Southeast Asian region. Refugees made their way to Singapore, Thailand, Hong Kong, Korea, Cambodia (Kampuchea), Malaysia, and the Philippines. During the month of August 1980, 6,204 Vietnamese arrived by boat in various Southeast Asian countries. At the same time, 11,832 Indochinese left camps in countries of first asylum for permanent resettlement in other countries (UNHCR 1981). Often the refugees were not certain as to their final destination and were initially interested in an immediate haven of safety (Liu and Marata 1977:44). From the Phillippines, many refugees traveled to Guam and made the trek from one camp to another prior to discovering their ultimate destination (see Figure 1).

Eventually, the people had two primary choices: immigrate to the United States (or a few other countries, e.g., Canada) or attempt repatriation into Vietnam. The majority chose the path of immigration and began to seek sponsorship in the United States.

1

Figure 1. From Vietnam to Camp Pendleton: A Survey
of fifty-nine families* included in a report to the
United States Congress, December 15, 1975, by the
Interagency Task Force for Indochina Refugees.

					No.	%
Singapore	Philippines	Guam	Wake Island	CP	10	16.9
	Philippines	Guam	Wake Island	CP	9	15.3
Vietnam	Philippines	Guam		CP	26	44.1
Thailand		Guam		CP	2	3.4
		Guam		CP	11	18.6
			Wake Island	CP	1	1.7
					59	100.0

Average Stay: Singapore and/or Thailand, 5 days
               the Philippines, 12 days
               Guam, 4 weeks
               Wake Island, 7 weeks

*The fifty-nine family units comprised 202 persons.

(Liu and Murata 1977)

The fall of the South was so sudden, that most countries were not prepared for the tremendous exodus from Vietnam which resulted in a need for resettlement in other nations. The United States set up staging areas on April 24, 1975, to assist and process the refugee population. Although the initial design was to relocate the Vietnamese in other countries, the unofficial policy of the United States permitted immigration by as many Vietnamese as desired entrance (Interagency Task Force 1975). Within a few months following the first major migration from Vietnam permanent residents had been accepted by the United States, Canada, France, Australia, the Philippines, and Taiwan (see Figure 2). Other countries had permitted Vietnamese entrance but in 1975 were continuing to admit the refugees on a temporary basis only. From April 1975 to December 1981, more than 600,000 refugees were accepted into sponsoring countries (see Figures 2, 3, and 4).

Figure 2.   Initial Refugee Total in Various Countries, 1975.

Country	Total
United States	6,588
Canada	3,926
France	1,836
Australia	158
Philippines	114
Taiwan	120

Liu and Murata, 1977.

Refugees, Not Immigrants

An important element in the Vietnamese flight from their homeland is the reality that they left as refugees and not as immigrants. Immigrants are persons who migrate from one geographical location to another on a voluntary basis (personal choice) and who, prior to that migration, have a destination in mind. From point of origin to place of arrival (ultimate) is normally a "single" journey from an immigrant without the trauma of an archipelago agenda while in transit. The refugee, on the other hand,

Figure 3. Locations of Resettlement of Indochinese Refugees May 1975 to December 1977.

Country	Population "accepted"
*United States	148,355
France	37,353
Canada	6,915
Australia	4,278
Malaysia	1,400
West Germany	961
Belgium	936
England	548
Denmark	522
New Zealand	466
Austria	233
Italy	214
Norway	196
Philippines	150
Netherlands	143
Switzerland	82
Israel	66
Total	202,844

Adapted from United States Congress Records, Senate (1978:27)

*As of December 1981, the official count of Indochinese Refugee arrivals in the United States was 565,757 (Refugee Reports, February letter; 8). This number also represents the estimated cumulative state totals from 1975 to 1981. See Figure 4 for Vietnamese population by state.

Figure 4. Refugee Arrival Data for the United States and Territories, and Estimated Cumulative State Totals to December 1981.

State	State Total	State	State Total
Alabama	2,409	Nevada	2,283
Alaska	459	New Hampshire	382
Arizona	3,798	New Jersey	5,108
Arkansas	2,594	New Mexico	2,940
California	192,105	New York	17,177
Colorado	9,014	North Carolina	4,589
Connecticut	5,289	North Dakota	626
Delaware	297	Ohio	7,318
District of		Oklahoma	7,171
Columbia	1,873	Oregon	16,509
Florida	9,889	Pennsylvania	21,412
Georgia	6,533	Rhode Island	3,439
Hawaii	6,230	South Carolina	2,137
Idaho	1,169	South Dakota	883
Illinois	21,306	Tennessee	3,274
Indiana	3,901	Texas	51,097
Iowa	8,370	Utah	7,179
Kansas	7,648	Vermont	299
Kentucky	2,007	Virginia	16,799
Louisiana	12,769	Washington	26,277
Maine	966	West Virginia	466
Maryland	6,185	Wisconsin	9,696
Massachusetts	11,062	Wyoming	424
Michigan	9,229	Guam	328
Minnesota	23,053	Puerto Rico	25
Mississippi	1,559	Unknown	21
Missouri	5,207	Virgin Islands	16
Montana	1,011		
Nebraska	1,970	Total.....565,757	

Source: Office of Refugee Resettlement/Department of Health and Human Services, and the Refugee Reports, 1982, American Council for Nationalities Service.

undertakes a forced migration toward an unknown destination and has numerous stops in route to resettlement. Kunz's theory of refugee flight and relocation is simple, but accurate. Once the initial flight has been set in motion, the refugee movement is shaped not by internal but rather by external forces acting upon it.

Specific characteristics of the Vietnamese refugees are also delineated by Kunz (in addition see UNHCR 1976; Tepper 1980; Whitemore 1980). The Vietnamese were an "acute" refugee movement, as opposed to "anticipatory" refugee movements. "Anticipatory" movements foresee a need to move and have enough lead time to prepare for resettlement in an orderly fashion. Refugees of "acute" movements are normally coerced into leaving through powerful military or political opponents and in a need to escape a given situation move quickly without the benefit of preparation. Therefore, in the moment of danger fleeing becomes the best possible solution. This response, however, normally results in regret at having left one's homeland, and often the desire to return remains strong.

A primary characteristic of the initial refugee population was its high level of education. According to most theories of refugee displacement, refugee populations tend to be more highly educated than the populace from which they emerged, and in the case of the Vietnamese this holds true. In the sample first taken by the Interagency Task Force of the United States Government, 72.4% of the refugees had completed at least one year of formal training in high school, and 18.9% had completed a portion of study on the university level (United States Department of State figures based on 114,140 refugees).

This education also reflects the economic stratification among many of the refugee people within their own country. The initial refugee population was primarily upper middle class with a median income of more than five times the median income of the country as a whole.

Preliminary Data

The studies undertaken at Camp Pendleton by Liu, Lamanna, and Murata involve a sample survey in order to secure preliminary data from the transitory refugee population. The results from a portion of the firstwave of refugees was as follows: (1) 96.5 percent of the sample had never resided outside Vietnam: (2) to most religion was a most important aspect of their lives; (3) close to one-half of the persons surveyed had been north of the 17th parallel in Vietnam, having fled to South Vietnam prior to 1975; (4) the age of the respondents was generally young with 30 percent under twenty years of age, 43 percent between twenty and forty years of age, 24 percent between forty and sixty years of age, and 3 percent over sixty years of age. (See Figures 5 and 6 for the survey results on religion.) (Liu, Lamanna, Murata, 1979:58-60.)

Therefore, the initial body of refugees was generally young, well educated, and belief (religious) oriented. Although they reveal a complexity which supersedes Kunz's general refugee profil, they were, nonetheless, entering the country as a secondary choice in response to circumstances beyond their control which threatened many of their lives.

The Processes of Adaptation

The Vietnamese entrance into the United States - a transition from one culture into a vastly different societal environment in a relatively brief period under "acute" circumstances - has provided an opportunity for investigation and understanding into the processes of adaptation one group makes in response to another. A common denomiator through which aspects of this process may be viewed is the institution of religion. Generally speaking, religion represents a basic and common value system for many of the Vietnamese people. Historically, Buddhism, Confucianism, and Taoism have combined to a form a unique Vietnamese philosophical and religious perspective (Brown 1981:5). In addition, Roman Catholicism has played a dynamic role among a smaller portion of the Vietnamese popultation, but, nonetheless, is highly represented among the Vietnamese in Oklahoma City. In a survey taken by the Vietnamese American Association in the Spring of 1980, 60 percent of the people identified themselves as Buddhist, 30 percent as Catholic, 10 percent as Christian, and a number identified themselves as holding animist views in addition to the above categories.

Figure 5.   Importance of Religion.

	Frequency	Percentage
Extremely Important	111	55.2%
Very Important	41	20.4
Moderately Important	30	14.9
Not so Important	15	7.5
Not Important at all	5	2.0
No answer	1	---
	202	100.0%

In the employment of religion and an examination of its role in the resettlement process, a model of ethnicity has emerged among the dynamics of culture contact as the best manner in which to understand the adaptive processes. Using as a background Barth, Schermerhorn, Despres, De Vos, Bennett, Hicks, and others, ethnicity is understood to be a process: active, creative, and dynamic. It is at times incorporated by one social unit in order to determine and/or fashion identity vis-a-vis another social group (unit), and is essentially a form of interaction between culture groups operating within common social contexts.

Data Gathered

Data was gathered during this study via personal interviews, participant observation, and archival research. Beginning as early as July 1980, more than 213 informal interviews were conducted over a period of twenty months. These interviews include a number of variables as to religion, age, sex, marriage relationship, length of residence in Oklahoma City, and professional status. Participant observation has ranged from participation in religious services to the personal instruction and demonstration of Buddhist religious practices by the Vietnamese Buddhist monks. Participation has also involved both large and small settings, formal and informal settings, as well as a variety of activities. In addition, information was provided by several of the larger sponsoring agencies of the Oklahoma City area. Among these were the Catholic Social Ministries, the Oklahoma Baptist Convention, the Vietnamese-American Association, and the Vietnamese Buddhist Temple of Oklahoma City.

Figure 6.   Religious Belief.

	Frequency	Percentage
Buddhist	55	27.2%
Catholic	111	55.0
Protestant	1	.5
Confucian	22	10.9
Other	1	.5
None	10	5.0
More than one religion	2	1.0
	202	100.0%

Oklahoma City

One of the primary centers for relocation and resettlement of the Vietnamese people in the United States is Oklahoma City. As of December 1981, the government estimated a total of over 7,000 Vietnamese in Oklahoma (ibid 1982:8). The Vietnamese people estimate a population of perhaps 12,000 or more, with an increase of between two and three hundred new persons each month to the city area.

Although the entrance of the Vietnamese into the United States, in general, and Oklahoma, in particular, is a relatively new phenomenon, much can be ascertained and understood even at this early date. It is the contention of this study that the Vietnamese of Oklahoma City in their adaptive processes employ religion as a primary factor of ethnic identity. This employment is utilized in both inter-ethnic encounters, as well as intra-ethnic relationship.

10

CHAPTER II

THE VIETNAMESE IN OKLAHOMA CITY

Settlement in Oklahoma City

The initial sponsorship program of the various Volunteer Agencies provided the catalyst for Vietnamese transition from the refugee camps to settlement in the United States. Having once entered the country, many Vietnamese people began to search for friends and relatives who had been located in adjoining or distant geographical areas. Movement to several major centers began, and many of the smaller isolated groups of Vietnamese began to relocate in major urban centers. One such urban center which has drawn the Vietnamese people is Oklahoma City.

There were several reasons for the choice of Oklahoma City. The climate is mild and the seasonal changes are not drastic. The employment opportunities in Oklahoma City were high. The close proximity to Fort Chaffee where many of the refugees had been located was also a positive factor as the move could be made with relative ease.

The influence of the medical center and the availability of Vietnamese doctors also played a prominent role. As explained by a Vietnamese businessman,

> I came to Oklahoma City because my son was here. He is a doctor and he said this was a good area. Also, there were other doctors here (Vietnamese) and so many other families came because of that. The climate is good. So we came over forty of us together.

Another Vietnamese store owner explained the decision to move to Oklahoma City in this manner:

> There was a doctor here who had been with the Saigon Medical School and he was very good. He got many other doctors to come here and their families. Some of their families wrote us and told us they were here and that they would come to the house to see us if we were sick. I like Viet-

11

namese doctors and I do not drive very good. I opened my store three years ago and now have many customers. This is a good place for us.

The Vietnamese who first came to Oklahoma City did not represent a cross section of Vietnamese society. More highly educated and more influential than the norm, they were some of the first to flee the Communist takeover of the Southern part of Vietnam. The first wave of Vietnamese immigrants to the United States, of which most of the original residents of Oklahoma City were a part, are generally characterized as highly professional and highly educated. In a recent study by Donald N. Brown the first wave was considered to have contained

a disproportionately large number of well educated individuals with medical, pro- fessional, technical and managerial job skills--over 31 percent of all refugee heads of households. Almost half of this group (47.8 percent) had completed secon- dary education and an additional 27.4 percent had completed university programs. Physicians were especially highly repre- sented among the refugees, with 660 of the 2,500 physicians in South Vietnam fleeing from their homeland. (Brown 1981:14)

The first people were also stronger economi- cally than subsequent waves of boat people, and often fled Vietnam for fear of religious perse- cution. As a Vietnamese-Catholic woman explains,

I am from Hanoi and I left there when the Communists took over. I went South and lived there until the United States troops left and then I came here. I was afraid of the Communists. I was afraid to be Catholic. Here I can be Catholic and Vietnamese, too.

Persons who were closely related to the United States government presence in South Vietnam also fled to America. A large number of government employees located in the Washington, D.C. or urban Virginia area, although a few of these employees came to Oklahoma City sponsored and/or encouraged by friends from Tinker Air Force Base.

12

The Vietnamese-American Association

One of the strongest aspects of Vietnamese relocation to Oklahoma City is the Vietnamese American Association. Located at 3121 North Classen Boulevard, the Association provides numerous services for the Vietnamese community. Funded by grants from the Department of Health, Education, and Welfare, the Association is led by Nguyen Dihn Thu, president. In a speech prepared and delivered by Nguyen Dinh Thu entitled, "The Vietnamese Refugees in Oklahoma City and Their Problems," the initial funding is explained:

> the Vietnamese American Association has been awarded uninterrupted grants by the Department of Health and Human Services (HEW) under the heading of English Language Development and Employment Services and Mental Health Projects during consecutive FY 1978-1979 and 1979-1980, and for the Fiscal year of 1980-1981, the Vietnamese American Association entered into contract with the Oklahoma State Department of Human Services for providing the Indochinese Refugee in the State of Oklahoma the English Language Development and Manpower Services and Social Adjustment Services.

The Association originated in the relocation camps. Several refugee persons started English language classes in the camp at Fort Chaffee, Arkansas, and continued the classes upon arrival in Oklahoma City. Chartered in late 1975 by a group of approximately eighty refugees as a Mutual Assistance Association (MAA), it was soon incorporated as the Vietnamese American Association, a publically supported non-profit organization. Since that time the Association (hence, VAA) has constructed a program of considerable variance.

Included in the VAA's program is a counseling center. The center is designed to assist in the sponsorship of refugee families, assist in the reunification of separated family members, provide orientation for new arrivals to the city, provide crisis counseling, and provide information on social, medical, and religious services available in the Oklahoma City area.

The VAA has also established a job placement service. The service provides career planning, as well as contacts with prospective employers. It educates the job-seeker on how to conduct one's self in an interview, and the cultural information he would need to make the best impression.

Another primary service of the VAA is "English as a Second Language" classes. Thirteen different classes are offered on several different levels. Since 1977, more than 2,000 people have enrolled in the classes, and currently the enrollment level is approximately 200.

Other regular services of the VAA include driving classes, a mass media program on radio station KSCS (FM 90.1) each Sunday in both Vietnamese and English, newsletters and announcements of special community events, and the maintenance and promotion of ethnic celebrations such as Tet, the Vietnamese New Year.

The VAA of Oklahoma City was the first of the Mutual Assistant Association's to receive a mental health grant from the American government. Although it is designed to serve the entire state of Oklahoma, its most notable work is performed with the sizeable Vietnamese population in Oklahoma City.

The Vietnamese-American Sponsorship

As the Vietnamese American Association became established, it initiated a program of sponsorship by Vietnamese families in Oklahoma City who could serve as sponsors for Vietnamese still in Fort Chaffee or other relocation camps. This program accelerated the size and growth of the Vietnamese population and proved to be another reason for the selection of Oklahoma City as an area for resettlement.

The sponsoring families assisted the new arrivals in several areas. First of all, they provided a residence on a temporary basis until permanent housing could be acquired. This residential status assisted in the search for employment as the new arrival projected a sense of permanency.

Often the sponsoring family was able to secure work for the new arrival at the place where the sponsor was employed. When this was possible, it eliminated transportation problems, as the workers traveled to and from work together.

Additionally, the Vietnamese sponsoring family served as a catalyst in the adjustment to a new set of customs both on the job and in the greater community. The setting of the Vietnamese home provided a reservoir of strength and communication as experiences were shared in a more familiar environment. This helped to alleviate some of the feeling of isolation which would be natural in such a resettlement process.

Characteristics of the Oklahoma City Population

The majority (58 percent) of the Vietnamese in Oklahoma City as of 1980 were under twenty-four years of age. A relatively young population, in general, only seven percent of the people were fifty-five years of age or older (see Figure 7).

The vast majority (74 percent) of the Vietnamese people indicate a religious preference for either Buddhism or Roman Catholicism. According to the Mental Health survey of 1978, 18 percent practice ancestor worship, 38 percent practice Catholicism, 36 percent practice Buddhism, 6 percent practice Protestantism in one form or another, and 2 percent preferred other religions.

Figure 7. Age Levels of Oklahoma City Vietnamese, 1980.

Years of Age	Percentage of Population
0-5	12%
6-10	11%
11-13	6%
14-24	29%
25-34	17%
35-44	10%
45-54	8%
55-64	3%
65 and up	4%
Total	100%

Source: 1980 Spring Survey. Vietnamese American Association, Oklahoma City.

Family Size

The 1980 survey indicated that the majority of Oklahoma City Vietnamese households were comprised of nuclear families. The extended family household units of three generations--grandparents, parents, and children--was very small as were the number of persons living alone (see Figure 8).

Figure 8. Family Organizations.

Family Size of One Household	Percentage
Nuclear family	57%
Extended families	12%
Single living	13%
Married with no children	8%
Married, residing with sibling's family	2%
Divorced with children	2%
Widowed with children	1%
Other	5%
Total	100%

Source: Compiled from the 1980 Spring Survey, Vietnamese American Association, Oklahoma City.

Occupational Characteristics and Changes

The Vietnamese in Oklahoma City have made significant progress in securing and maintaining employment. Often a Vietnamese person who was skilled in English was placed in a strategic job market. Following a few weeks or months of employment, the employer was approached concerning vacancies within the business or corporation which could be filled by members of the Vietnamese community who were not fluent in the English language. Based both on the performance level of the existing Vietnamese employee, and the ability of that employee to serve as an interpreter, many other Vietnamese people were hired by Oklahoma City merchants. The new positions resulted in occupational change for many, of the refugee people in Oklahoma City. Previously, in Vietnam, most of the individuals had been government or military employees (54 percent), but in the relocation

16

process similar employment was not possible. Figure 9 details the occupational change from Vietnam to the United States for the year 1977 and 1980.

Figure 9. Occupational Changes.

Category	Vietnam	Okla. City 1977	Okla. City 1980
Military	32%	0%	0%
Government Employees	22%	0%	0%
Business (Private)	14%	2%	2%
Clerical	12%	14%	12%
Skilled Worker	5%	52%	64%
Laborers	8%	25%	12%
Students	7%	2%	2%
Unemployed	0%	5%	8%

Source: Compiled from the 1980 Spring Survey, Vietnamese American Association, Oklahoma City.

Survival in the relocation process has necessitated changes in employment. For instance, one Vietnamese man, formerly the equivalent of a United States Senator in South Vietnam, has developed a yard service with the assistance of his two teenage sons. Another man, formerly a high ranking government official in South Vietnam, works as a custodian for a local Baptist Church. In both cases, employment equal in either status or pay to that held in Vietnam was not possible in the United States.

Economic Strength

The Vietnamese community of Oklahoma City may be characterized by its economic gains from 1975 to 1980. Results of a survey taken by the VAA of one hundred families comparing their economic strength

from 1977 to 1980 provided the following information: (1) 32 percent of the families were earning
approximately $1,000 per month in 1977 and by 1980
the percentage had risen to 64 percent; (2) the
percentage of families earning $500 or less declined
from 26 percent to less than 10 percent; (3) the
percentage of female employment in the Vietnamese
community rose steadily each year, with only 13
percent of the Vietnamese adult women considering
themselves to be full-time housewives in 1980; (4)
the families with two or more family members
employed increased from 45 percent to 55 percent.

Housing

Concurrent with the increased employment of the
Vietnamese community has been the increasing number
of home purchases. In 1977, twenty-three percent of
the people were purchasing their own homes. By
1980, the percentage had doubled to forty-six
percent and the number of renters had declined from
seventy-seven percent to fifty-four percent. This
ability to make major purchases is increased
evidence of the economic progress of the Oklahoma
City Vietnamese.

Transportation

The adjustment to Oklahoma City has included
transportation. The city does not provide any
comprehensive public transports--subways, rapid
transit--and individual travel is still the primary
means of transportation.

Reflecting this need, the Vietnamese family has
actively acquired additional automobiles. In 1977,
thirty-six percent of the families owned and
operated two or more automobiles purchased within
the United States. By 1980, almost one-half (49%)
of the families operated two or more cars and
purchases were on the increase. According to one
Vietnamese man, car sharing (car pooling) was not
possible since different family members required
transportation to various places at various times.

Assistance Utilized

The use of government economic assistance programs in 1980 reflects the economic adaptability of the Vietnamese people. The largest majority of the community (72%) was not receiving any monetary assistance. Of the remaining 28 percent, five percent were receiving food stamps, two percent were receiving financial aid assistance for higher education, nine percent were receiving direct cash benefits, and nine percent were receiving medical subsidies. The usage of food stamps, for instance, had dropped four percent from 1977 to 1980 (see Figure 10).

Figure 10. Government Assistance

Type	Percentage 1977	Percentage 1980
No assistance	72%	72%
Food stamps	9%	5%
Unemployment	0%	3%
Medical Subsidies	9.5%	9%
Financial Adi, College or University	0%	2%

Source: Compiled from the 1980 Spring Survey, Vietnamese American Association, and interviews with Nguyen Dinh Thu, President, Vietnamese American Association, Oklahoma City.

Public Opinion

Prior to the Vietnamese entrance into Oklahoma, neither the Sooner state nor Oklahoma City had a history of Asian settlement. The Vietnamese relocation in Oklahoma City was a new phenomenon for the state.

Unique to the settlement process was the absence of negative stories in the local newspapers.

That is not to say that the newcomers were welcomed with open arms. Instead, there seemed to be a basic ambilvalence which continues to be undefined.

That in itself may have proven to be a catalyst for increasing numbers of Vietnamese people to gravitate toward the Oklahoma City urban center. While New Orleans, New York, and areas of Southern California painted a negative portrait of the Vietnamese people (Department of State "Indochinese Resettlement in America" 1977), Oklahoma City greeted the arrivals with media silence. Isolated reports appeared in the papers, but negative campaigns were never mounted.

Concurrent with the media "neutrality" was the positive assistance of some community leaders, churches, public health officials, and volunteers from Tinker Air Force Base. Assistance was provided in order to better facilitate the adjustment process. Neither overwhelmingly positive or negative, the initial general opinion appeared to be one of passivity.

Mental Health Problems

On October 3, 1980, the VAA hosted an "Indochinese Refugee Resettlement Seminar." Among the speakers were Dao The Xuong, M.D., Mental Health Project Director; Carol Sedanko, an administrator from the Social Services Regional Office in Dallas, Texas; John Searle, Chief Administrator of the Stae of Oklahoma Resettlement Department; Nguyen Dinh Thu, President, Vietnamese American Association; and Vuong G. Thuy, author of Getting to Know the Vietnamese and Their Culture.

Discussions centered on: (1) the depression generated by the knowledge that family members remained in Vietnam; (2) the anxiety resulting in the loss of societal status; (3) the homesick nature of many of the refugee people resulting from the sudden and relatively unplanned departure from Vietnam; and (4) religion as a primary element of mental health.

Of the Vietnamese in Oklahoma, almost half (47 percent) reported depression or anxiety related to family members still in Vietnam. Almost 40 percent reported a feeling of homsickness, and many others expressed difficulty in adjusting to the new and alien culture.

The Established Vietnamese Community

The Vietnamese community in 1982 is an established part of Oklahoma City. Numbering between 7,100 and 12,000 the Vietnamese continue to grow in number and strength. Vietnamese food stores and fish markets are now prominent in Oklahoma City. Restaurants serving Chinese and Vietnamese cuisine are reaching beyond the Vietnamese community and increasing their clientele in the Anglo communities. Tailoring shops have been opened along with stores featuring fine jewelry and ceramic products. A Buddhist temple has been established and is currently in a building program. The Vietnamese Catholic community worships regularly in an older established Catholic church with the aid of a Vietnamese priest. Real estate agents, physicians, and many other professional fields are represented among the people.

Concurrent with the development of their own community, there is an expanded effort to share the Vietnamese culture with the other residents of the city. Tet, the Vietnamese New Year, is actively promoted to include persons outside the Vietnamese community. Neighbors in the community where the Buddhist temple is located have been invited to displays of the martial arts by the Buddhist monks, and the VAA has offered to provide a list of tutors to persons desiring to learn the Vietnamese language.

Continuing Needs

Although the Vietnamese are continuing to grow economically and numerically, their problems are not yet fully solved. Intangible problems continue to persist. Problems involving members separated from the immediate family, and involving the establishment of an ethnic identity within a new society continue to cause concern among the Vietnamese people.

Problems related to fluency in English continue to plague many Vietnamese. A generation gap between teenagers who are acquiring more American traits and the older generation which wants to maintain Vietnamese values has become a problem for many families. Probably the most wide-spread and significant problems, however, are related to homesickness and depression. A survey by the Vietnamese Mental Health Project indicated that only 14 percent were only slightly depressed about family members still living in Vietnam, while 86 percent were either very depressed or moderately depressed. In another question, 46 percent of the respondents reported feeling very alone in the United States and only 17 percent reported that they felt "not at all" alone. (Brown 1981:21).

As material needs are being more fully met, attention is beginning to focus more directly on the emotional and cultural aspects of the Vietnamese adjustment to the United States.

CHAPTER III

TRADITIONAL VIETNAMESE RELIGIONS

In order to understand the Vietnamese people, it is necessary to understand both the content and the role of Vietnamese religions. Religion is central to Vietnamese philosophy, social behavior, and ethnic awareness. It permeates every institution--political, cultural, theological--and remains central to the Vietnamese people even within the framework of a new society. It serves as a catalyst for ethnic self-identification, and as such is a key factor in the adaptation process.

The Study of Religion

The study and examination of religion or religions requires a multiplicity of tools. Since religions invariably reflect human experience and understanding, the study of religion encompasses history, ethnology, linguistics, literaure, philosophy, economics, sociology, political science, and anthropology.

Among the "Great Religions" of the world may be discovered repetition and similarity, as well as variations and significant differences. This similarity becomes clear when it is understood that of the five great religions--Judaism, Christianity, Islam, Hinduism, Buddhism--a reduction to two may be made historically. Hinduism and Judaism may be considered the genesis of the other three: Hinduism as the seed ground for Buddhism; Judaism, for Christianity and Islam.

The differences between the two major traditions may be viewed from a philosophical perspective as a springboard to theological developments. For instance, there is a fundamental difference in the way time is perceived. The Western orientation of linear time is countered by the Eastern orientation of cyclical time. In addition there is a vast gulf between the East and West in the perception of life. For the Western mind, generally speaking, life is good. To extend life is a positive course and a course to be desired leading to the conceptualization of an after life. To the Eastern mind, generally speaking, life is bad and the natural course is for one to seek escape from life. Subsequently, there is, generally speaking, no highly developed eschatology for Eastern religions. Instead, one is offered an escape from perpetual or eternal existence, and Nirvana becomes a mystical union with the universe, not an extension of life.

Inherent also in the study of religion is the cultural diversity of the native society which has shaped the contents of the religion's dogma and practice. In order to better understand religion or a religion, it must be studied in the framework of the greater society (see Figure 11).

The Place of Religion

Although there are variations among the Vietnamese people--according to provincial backgrounds and/or regional nuances--religious values have served as a foundation for basic value orientation. Confucianism, Taoism, and Buddhism were all external influences which merged with an indigenous form of ancestor worship to produce a remarkable Vietnamese religious orientation (Hickey 1964, Thuy 1976, Whitemore 1979, Brown 1981).

Buddhism was introduced into Vietnam by Indian and Chinese traders (Cady 1967). The influence was predominantly Chinese and the Buddhist school most prominent was the Mahayana School (northern school); a minority of Vietnamese practice Theravada Buddhism (southern school).

Confucianism, more a religious philosophy than a religion per se, has influenced both the culture and the human development of Vietnam. Introduced to the region in the eleventh century, Confucianism addressed itself to the maintenance of social and family order. For Confucius (K'ung Fu Tzu or Master Kung), the main ethics of life are Jen, benevolence or humanity, and Shu, tolerance or reciprocity. The four classes of society were: (1) the intelligentsia, (2) the peasants, (3) the craftsmen, and (4) the merchants. The ethical instruction--faith for society and the home-- centered on filial piety and altruism. It was important to recognize rank (age and relationship) within the family and within the society. One was to honor first the king, secondly, the teacher, and thirdly, the father in a predescribed hierarchical pattern.

Figure 11. Cross-Cultural Differences Between East and West.

	West	East
Religion	Montheistic	Pantheistic, Polytheistic, Spiritualistic, Humanistic
Culture	Christian	Hinduist, Buddhist, Confucianist, Taoist
Civilization	Industrial (man over nature, development of science and technology)	Agricultural (harmony between man and nature, little development of science and technology)
Philosophy	Speculative	Contemplative
Philosophy of Life	Materialistic Individualism	Self-realization (The moral self) Altruism
	Achievement, power prestige	Mutual dependence, love for all men
	Individual autonomy, competition, aggression	Reconciling and harmonizing tendencies
	Activity	Living more with the past
	Future orientation	Esteem for hierarchy Esteem for nature

Adapted from Tran Van Mai. "Cross-Cultural Understanding and its Implications in Counseling." Printed in "Indochinese Health Care." A Conference for Health Professionals, San Diego, California, November 27, 1979.

25

Taoism was another of many outside influences reaching Vietnam from China. The principle teachings of Taoism are charity, simplicity, patience, contentment, and harmony (between people and between humankind and nature). In the interest of harmony, Taoism teaches that all forms of confrontation should be avoided. Taoism, unlike Confucianism, had developed a professional religious body (priests) and temple worship centers. This organization did not, however, penetrate Vietnam and remains, for the Vietnamese, primarily a "philosophical" orientation (Brown 1981:6). The philosophy of Taoism, along with Buddhist (Four Noble Truths, Eight-fold Path) and Confucian admonitions (filial peity, loyalty, wisdom, honesty), have integrated to deeply affect the Vietnamese culture, ideology, and consequently, Vietnamese behavior (see Figure 12).

In addition to Asian belief systems, Roman Catholicism entered Vietnam through outside influences. In the sixteenth century, Portugese missionaries first entered Vietnam to be followed later by the Spanish and French. The religion grew rapidly in the seventeenth and eighteenth centuries, and by the mid-twentieth century Roman Catholics counted seventeen million adherents to their church. Although it was not as widespread as the Asian religions, and certainly not as old, Roman Catholicism affected both the political and social life of the people. Many of the refugees who came into the United State in 1975 and following were members of the Roman Catholic Church.

Confucianism

The ethical system referred to as Confucianism originated with the Revered Master, K'ung Fu Tzu. The Chinese name for the Confucianism school is Ju Chiao or "the School of the Scholars." Its philosophy has been a major influence in Chinese educational, political, and cultural development. Extending from China, Confucianism has also influenced the social structures of Korea, Japan, and Vietnam.

The life of Confucius. The traditionally accepted dates of Confucius' life are 551-479 B.C. Raised as a commoner in an impoverished environment, he was married at the age of nineteen and soon

Figure 12. Vietnamese Religious Philosophy.

Item	Americans	Vietnamese
Human nature orientation	Human nature is basically evil but perfectible.	Human nature is basically good but corruptible.
Man - nature orientation	Mastery over nature	Harmony between man and nature
Time orientation	Living with future time	Living with the past
Space orientation	Living with movement, migration, and mobility	Attached to nature or ancestor land - immobile
Activity orientation	Doing, getting things done	Being-in-becoming
Relation orientation	Individual autonomy, self-reliance	Lineality, mutual dependence

Adapted from Nguyen Quoc Tri. "Culture and Technical Assistance in Public Administration. A Study of What Can Be Transferred from the United States to Vietnam." Unpublished doctoral dissertation, University of Southern California, 1970.

27

thereafter fathered a son. Shortly after his son's birth, he divorced his wife and began to travel. At this point, legend varies, but most legends speak of K'ung as an itinerant teacher and a government employee.

During these years of employment, from approximately age 20-55, Confucius developed a system of philosophical perspectives on life and government. During the later years of his life he traveled around the countryside expounding his philosophy and developing disciples. Before his death, he returned to his native province and established a school for his followers. It was through this school that Confucius presented his social system in written form and established a base for the continuation of his "religion" following his death.

The Confucian scriptures. Although there is some debate concerning the exact authorship of Wa Ching (Five Classics) and the Shu Shu (Four Books), these writings are generally accepted as the basic Confucian scriptures. The Wa Ching is considered a personal work of K'ung, while the Shu Shu is a commentary on Confucius by a number of his followers.

The five classics credited to Confucius are the Shu Ching (Book of History), the Shih Ching (Book of Poetry), the I Ching (Book of Changes), the Li-Chi (Book of Rites), and the Ch'un Ch'iu (Spring and Autumn Annals). Depending on one's interpretation, a sixth book is sometimes added, the Hsiao Ching (Book of Filial Piety). The Classics run the gamut from ancient chronicles and traditions, to commentary on systems of the social order and education. The four books by K'ung's followers include the Lun-Yu (Discourses of Confucius), the Ta-Hsueh (Great Learning), the Chung Yung (Central Harmony), and the Meng Tee (Book of Mencius). The books contain not only essential information on the life and teachings of Confucius, but also an extensive elaboration of his teachings by his closest disciples, particularly Mencius.

The world view of Confuciansim. The basic tenets of Confuciansim are found in his basic principles of life. Viewed by some as a religion and by other as a system of political and social thought, Confucius has had a startling impact on the concepts of many of the world's people.

Confucius taught that humankind is basically good. Unfortunately, humans have not developed the nature of their goodness, and therefore, need to be educated in the place of virtue('s). The failure of humankind to develop their goodness created disharmony within society and within relationship. Both heaven and earth were infected by this disharmony.

The solution according to Confucius was to return to the ways of the ancestors. A study of the classics would provide the return to virtue and to a golden age of ideal harmony. The foundation of harmony is found in filial piety, Hsiao, Shu, and Li. Filial piety is a hierarchy of relationships involving son to father, wife to husband, younger brother to elder brother, servant to master, and citizen to emperor. In each case the subordinate person expresses Hsiao (respect and obedience) to the superior. Shu is the essence of Confucian's teaching, "What you do not want done to yourself, do not do to others" (Lun Yu 15:23). Li, or propriety, is the way of right conduct, and became the principle method "face-saving" behavior.

Political and social influence. Confucius teachings emphasized the reconstruction of the past, not the anticipation of the future. When a disciple inquired as to K'ung's perception of death, he replied, "Why do you ask me about death when you do not know about life?"

In this treatment of "knowing life" Confucius' contribution centered on the idea that nobility rose out of character, not out of the circumstances of birth. This nobility, evident in filial piety, revolutionized the place of the family. Not only was obedience required to one's living superiors, but respect for one's ancestors was generated into the past by means of ancestor worship (veneration). As a projection of this concept, the future required sons in order that one's own immortality could be preserved. The Confucian temples soon became the storehouses of ancestor tablets where an individual went to discuss with the ancestors the circumstances of one's life. This loyalty to family superceded all else, including loyalty to the elements of government.

Taoism

The religious philosophy of Taoism is attributed to Lao Tzu who was born in approximately 604 B.C. Referred to as the "old master" and the founder of Taoism, the school of thought did not gain prominence until the fourth century B.C. under the leadership of Chuang Tzu.

The life of Lao Tzu. The details of Lao Tzu's life are difficult to document accurately. Other than his birth during the early part of the sixth century B.C., little is known of his life. It is generally believed that he became disillusioned with his own society and departed to be a wandering sage. So great was his disillusionment that he decided to disappear from his "world." Tradition states that prior to his journey, a friend pleaded with him to put his thoughts in writing. This he did, in the Way-Virtue-Classic, and then vanished somewhere in the area of Central Asia.

The writings of Lao Tzu. The Tao Teh Ching (classic of the way of virtue) or Way-Virtue-Classic is the book written by Lao Tzu at the insistence of his friend. The writing is a compilation of eighty-one poems on the significance and essence of Tao. Simple in language, but complex in meaning, the Tao Teh Ching is considered to be the original source of Taoist teachings.

The world view of Taoism. Taoism emphasizes a return to the simplicity of nature. The emphasis centers on a personal search for the Tao (the natural way): the eternal, impersonal, mystical, supreme principle that lies behind the universe. The symbol of yang and yin are primary. Representing the two basic interacting modes of what "is," yang is masculine, active, warm, dry and positive; while yin is feminine, dark, cold, inactive and negative. Everything that "is" (humans, spirits, the world) exists through the dynamic interaction of these two forces. Tao teaches the need for humans to follow the natural way, and cease trying to improve through society-made legislation.

Taoism as a folk religion. The philosophy of Taoism has, since the fourth century B.C., been superceded by a mystical superstition which many scholars believe was never intended by Lao Tzu. Its practice was characterized by superstition, magical incantations, witchcraft, animism, astrology, demonism, and ancestor worship.

Buddhism

Although Vietnam is in southeast Asia geographically, religiously it has been more closely linked with China in East Asia. Accordingly, the Buddhist influence has been Mahayana as opposed to Theravada which is predominant in most of Southeast Asia. Prior to the communist unification of the northern and southern regions of Vietnam in 1975, up to seventy percent of the Vietnamese population was considered Buddhist.

The life of Gautama and the beginning of Buddhism. In the general development of Buddhism one can clearly see the effects of the Eastern mind. Founded by Siddhartha Gautama (560-480 B.C.) a prince of a Hindu caste, Buddhism reflects the conceptualization of life as a burden to be discarded or overcome.

At twenty-nine years of age, Gautama identified the burden of life in the twofold problem of sin and suffering. Seeking an answer to this dilemma he attempted philosophical speculation without successfully reaching a conclusion. He, therefore, decided to undertake the path of bodily asceticism (Gaer 1967:167). After five years of searching he decided to decreate the intensity of his asceticism and still continue along this general path. At thirty-five, while seated under the bo tree (bodhi) in meditation, he experienced enlightenment and became the Buddha, the enlightened one (Latorette 1956:91). During the remainder of his life he taught others concerning the Middle Path to Enlightenment. This enlightenment would lead to Nirvana, the place of freedom from rebirth. Siddhartha Gautama died at the age of eighty.

Following his death, the Buddha's disciples organized into a sangha (religious order) with definite rules and schedules. These rules necessitated a yellow robe, a shaven head, daily meditations, and affirmation of the Three Refuges. It was agreed that Refuge was to be found in the Buddha, the dharma (law-doctrine), and in the sangha.

In addition, ten negative precepts had to be followed. These precepts taught abstinence from destroying life, stealing, lying, committing adultery, drinking intoxicants, eating at forbidden times, dancing and attending theatricals, adorning oneself, having large beds, and possessing gold or silver (Parrinder 1964:144).

Essential features of Buddhism. One of the primary features of the Middle Path to salvation from rebirth involves true knowledge of the Four Noble Truths. These truths are: (1) existence (life) is suffering, (2) suffering is caused by inherently insatiable desires, (3) desire must be suppressed in order to end suffering and existence, (4) the way to achieve this is to follow the Eightfold Path (Ashby 1955:35ff). The Eightfold Path entails right views, right aims or intentions, right speech, right action, right livelihood, self-discipline, self-mastery, and contemplation. These eight mandates form the core of the Buddha's teachings, and may be found in his early sermons, as well as in the Tripitaka.

The Buddhist scriptures. The Tripitaka ("Three Baskets") is the basic scripture of Buddhists transmitted orally from the Buddha's time in the Pali language. The Three Baskets are the Vinaya, containing monastic rules; the Sutra, teachings of the Buddha; and Adhidharma, metaphysical commentaries on the Sutra (Gard 19674:127ff).

The two main schools of Buddhism. The two main schools of Buddhism are the Hinayana (Theravada) and Mahayana schools. The Hinayana or "lesser vehicle" (tradition) is the older of the two schools and closer to the teachings of the Buddha. The Mahayana or "greater vehicle" (tradition) is the newer of the two schools and is distinguished by its adaptability and departure from the original tenets.

There are other distinctions worth noting. For instance, the Hinayana or Theravada school is found predominantly in Southeast Asia: Ceylon, Burma, Thailand, Cambodia, Laos, and to some small degree in Vietnam; hence, the name, the Southern school. The Mahayana school is denoted the Northern school as it is predominant in Japan, Korea, China, Nepal, Tibet, and Vietnam (Starkes 1978:48).

Their separation, however, is not solely geographical. The Theravada Buddhists adhere to the teachings prescribed by the original Buddha and his immediate followers. In Theravada Buddhism, the historical Buddha is the only Buddha. Mahayanists recognize the historical Buddha as only one Buddha in a long chain of Buddha manifestations. The various Buddhas, according to Mahayanists, have had different teachings and the whole of these teachings are accepted as scripture. This leads to a variety of Mahayana "denominations" depending on the particular scriptural teachings which are emphasized (Swearer 1970:196).

Other distinctions include:

THERAVADA	MAHAYANA
1. A reverent attitude toward relics and images of the Buddha.	1. Buddha is considered the supreme Reality, or an incarnate savior (emphasis found in late Sunskrit scriptures). Buddha is the essence of existence.
2. Monasteries are frequented by monks and laypeople who periodically enter to live.	2. There are innumerable bodhisattvas; persons who have attained nirvana but postpone entrance in order to aid others.
3. Includes many lesser deities depending on the country in which it resides.	3. Heaven and hell are often vividly portrayed.
4. The worship of the Buddha is merely an commemoration.	4. The Buddha himself is a personification of the law.
5. Religion is a full time job (thus for monks).	5. Religion relevant to life in the world (thus for laymen, too).
6. Humankind as an individual.	6. Humankind as involved with others.

7. Humankind on their own in the universe (salvation by self-effort).	7. Humankind not along (salvation by grace; by faith in the Budhisattva).
8. Norm: Buddha's teachings.	8. Norm: Buddha's life of Compassion.
9. Ideal: the Arahat (Monk).	9. Ideal: the Bodhisattva (a holy person who has vowed not to enter Nirvana until whole human race has achieved salvation).
10. Key Virtue: Wisdom	10. Key Virtue: Compassion (Karuna).
11. Buddha: a saint.	11. Buddha: a savior.
12. No metaphysics.	12. Elaborate metaphysics.
13. Little ritual.	13. Includes ritual.
14. Confines prayer to meditation.	14. Includes petitionary prayer.
15. Has definite canan of scriptures, Tipitaka: "The Three Baskets": a. Sutta - teaching basket - teachings, sermons, dialogues of Buddha. b. Vinaya - 227 rules for monks. c. Abhidhamma - special Dhamma section, very advanced psychology.	15. Has no canonical scripture. Classic text is Lotus Sutra: "Lotus of the Good Law."

The adaptability of Buddhism. Owing to Buddhism's practice of syncretism, it has proved to be highly adaptable. Buddhists can include a variety of beliefs and practices of other religions within their lifestyle and continue to be Buddhist. For instance, one may practice Taoist beliefs within one's

34

profession, follow Confucian teachings in one's social relationships, and simultaneously practice Buddhism at weddings, funerals, and other ceremonial events. This is not to indicate, however, that Buddhism is without basic tenets. In fact, three of the major Mahayana schools--The Pure Land, Zen, Niciren--advocate primary teachings as central to their particular belief system.

The Mahayana schools. The Pure Land School has historically been found primarily in China and Japan. Central to this school of thought is Amida, or Amitabha, a Buddha who presides over the Pure Land, or Western Paradise. Entrance into the "Land" is premised on faith in Amida, not on good works. Consequently, regulations regarding behavior are not as developed as the Hinayana school. Clergy, for instance, live among the people, as opposed to isolated separation from the world.

Zen Buddhism, the intuitive school, is known as Ch'an in China and Vietnam. Rigidly individualistic, Zen produces no temples or images and advocates simple living and self discipline. Salvation comes from within as the true Buddha nature is within the heart of humankind. Reason proves to be of little worth to Zen Buddhist. Instead, the method of enlightenment is Zagen (a form of meditation similar to yogic in Hinduism) and the goal of Zen is satori, a flash of intuition such as experienced by Gautama.

Nichiren Buddhism, unlike the Pure Land School and Zen, believes that salvation is to be found only in the Lotus Sutra, a Sanskrit scripture often referred to as the "Gospel of the Pure Land." Extremely nationalistic, Nichiren has numerous off-spring including the Buddhist school of Soka Gakkai.

Christianity

Christianity is a combination of two major traditions. Originating within Judaism, Christianity arose from a Jewish heritage and expanded into a world dominated by a Greek mentality. The combinations of these two traditions form the matrix of the Christian religion today.

The life of Jesus. Born approximately 5-3 B.C., Jesus was a carpenter's son in Nazareth of Jewish origin. His life is relatively unknown until the age

Figure 13.

BUDDHISM
(Initial and General Development)

HINAYANA

MAHAYANA

Theravada

Sarrastivda

Sautrantika

Yogacara
(Idealism)

Madhyamika
(Transcendentalism)

Jodo
(Chinese: Ching-tu)

Zen (Syncretistic)
(Chinese and Vietnamese
Ch'an)

Pure Land School

"sudden
illumination"

"gradual
enlightenment

of thirty when he began to teach publicly. Gathering
a small group of followers, Jesus taught that he,
himself, is the Son of God through whom salvation
comes by personal belief. After a three year public
life, Jesus was crucified by the Roman government in
Judea. Three days following his crucifixion, his
followers believed that Jesus returned to live again
as proof of his divinity.

The Christian scriptures. The Christian scriptures are normally divided into two parts. The first
part, or Old Testament, is a revelation of Yahweh's
covenant with the Israelite people. The second part,
or New Testament, is a partial record of the life of
Jesus, and a commentary on Jesus' teachings as they
pertain to the growth of the early Christian Church.
Jesus, himself, did not leave any teachings in
written form, and the gospels of the New Testament
are the writings of his disciples.

The world view of Christianity. Christianity
centers upon the plight of humankind and the response
of God to that plight. Humankind is perceived as
being a creation of God who gives humans the freedom
to obey or diobey their maker. Due to humankind's
choice of disobedience, humans are in need of
redemption. Unable to redeem one's self through good
works, knowledge, etc., humankind has been given
Jesus, the Son of God, who takes humankind's
punishment upon himself by dying on a cross. For
salvation, each person must accept this act of Jesus
in their behalf, and express, personally, their faith
in Jesus as the Messiah.

As a result, the Christian is exalted to live a
life of obedience in gratitude to God for one's
salvation. Combining the ethical nature of Judaism
and the teachings of the Hellinistic philosophers,
Christianity presents a highly developed system of
ethical behavior. This system provides the lifestyle expected of the believer who then views the
world as an temporary residence. One's permanent
residence is to be found in heaven--a place of
eternal existence prepared for the followers of
Jesus. The eschatology of Christianity, in comparison to other religions, holds a place of great
prominence (see Figure 14 for a comparison).

Figure 14. Chart Comparing Christian and Buddhist Beliefs.

Subject	Southern Buddhism	Northern Buddhism	Christianity
The Human Problem	Suffering		Sin, rebellion against the creator
Man/Woman	No-self		Unique personal being made in image of God
Founder	Gautama, in India		Jesus, of Bethlem
Life's Goal	Attainment of Nirvana		Heaven, communion with God
Sin	External Acts		Internal Disposition and External Acts
Buddha	Saint	Savior	World Religion Founder but not worshipped
Jesus	Teacher	Possible Possessor of Buddhahodd	Unique incarnation of God, Savior, worshipped
Supreme Being	Existence Irrelevant	Buddha	God in Christ, Christian Trinity
Salvation	Humankind Saves Itself	Faith in Buddha	Repentance and Faith in Christ
Life Beyond Death	None	Pure Land: Heaven with Amida Buddha	External life with God forever
Chief Virtue	Wisdom	Compassion	Love

The Political-Religious Groups of Vietnam

The Vietnamese people have, historically, possessed a "'le gaut du mervieilleux,' a certain proclivity for the supernatural" (Fall 1955:235) which has manifested itself in various religious movements. Two of these movements, each of which has exerted both political and military influence, are Cao-Dai, and Hoa-Hao.

Cao-Dai

Cao-Dai, known in Vietnamese as Dai Dao Tam Ky Pho Do (third amnesty of God) is a blend of Buddhism, Confucianism, Taoism and Catholicism. Premised on the belief that Cao-Dai is the heart of the universe and the Father of all human beings, Cao-Dai divides history into three major periods of revelation (see Figure 15).

These periods are evidence of spiritual evolution. In the first two periods God reveals truth through human servants. In the West, God's word is delivered by Moses and Jesus. In the East, God's word is delivered by Buddha and Lao Tze. The third amnesty, in which the present world has resided since 1925, is the era of God's word being dissiminated through spiritualism--a hierarchy of spiritualists (from the Pope to local mediums) and various categories of spirits.

Politically active and militarily potent (Cao-Dai advocated the arming of its two million followers for civil conflict in 1955), Cao-Dai has traditionally been anti-communist (ibid. 243). Presently, its strength and viability is difficult to assess since the fall of Saigon in 1975.

Hoa-Hao

The Phat Giao Hoa-Hao, or Hoa-Hao, began in 1939 in Vietnam as a form of Buddhist "protestantism." With more than a million and a half followers and located predominantly in the Mekong Delta, Hoa-Hao had a decidedly nationalistic character buoyed by an anti-French sentiment.

Figure 15.   The Three Major Revelatory Periods.

Period		Revelation Agents
1st	Buddhism	Nhiem Dang Co Phat
	Taoism	Thai Thuong Dao Quan
	Confuciansim	Phue Hi
	Christianity	Moses
2nd	Buddhism	Sakyamuni
	Taoism	Lao Tze
	Confuciansim	Confucius
	Christianity	Jesus Christ
	Islam	Mohammed
3rd	Caodaism	Spirit-beings

Source: Victor L. Oliver, Caodai Spiritism. Brill, Netherlands, 1976, p. 9.

Unlike Cao-Dai, Hoa-Hao does not combine all religions into one. Its teachings include the veneration of its founder, Huyah Phu So, and a highly disciplined personal prayer life (four prayers a day). Extremely puritanical in nature, the religion opposes elaborate ritual of any kind, and instead advocates prayer and meditation. Also, unlike Cao-Dai, it has not erected temples, and does not employ official liturgies.

Conclusion

During a presentation at the "Indochinese Refugee Resettlement Seminar," Vuong Gia Thuy, professor at Temple University, stated the following:

> "In order to understand the Indochinese, one has to understand his religion. The Vietnamese is influenced by three primary factors: Tao metaphysical philosophy, Buddhist concept of reincarnation, Confucian ethical and social rules. Vietnamese Christianity is open to Christianity for survival, but not open to all the religious beliefs. For instance, it does not adopt Christian moral values, it retains its own." (IRRS 1980)

Religion in Vietnam has historically played a prominent role in the development of the nation, as well as in the lives of individual Vietnamese families.

CHAPTER IV

ETHNICITY, A MODEL FOR DEVELOPING SELF-IDENTITY

The Vietnamese in Oklahoma City are a culturally displaced people. Their traditional cultural institutions differ dramatically from those of their host culture. Problems indigenous to cultural integration are often expressed in mental disorders (Aylesworth 1978:8) and extreme depression. Developing strategies to cope with the phenomenon of cultural displacement, the Vietnamese have been fashioning a self-identity of their own within the host culture. This identity is predicated upon ethnicity and is often employed through the religions of the Oklahoma City Vietnamese and the practices germane to those religions. This employment is based upon a concept of ethnicity designed not to preserve the past, but rather to fashion and maintain a host cultural identity.

Aspects of Culture Contact

The contact between two cultures resulting in cultural change and/or cultural retrenchment assumes interaction between the two cultural components. Although the variety of reactions are numerous, sociologists have historically identified four basic factors in every instance of culture contact (Lee 1969:220). These four factors are: the disintegration of the social order of the newly arrived cultural unit, the mixture of racial groups via reproduction, the fusion of cultures, and the initial disorganization of individual personalities within the contact situation.

These factors are premised on the belief that from the beginning of culture contact there is a transferring and blending of the two cultures. Variations of degree are evident in relation to the militaristic nature of the dominant group. Blending occurs more naturally between two similar cultures on friendly relations, but may also occur within the extreme circumstance of hostility, dominance, and cultural exploitation of one group by another although the process is slower, and the degree of transfer lessened.

43

A Brief Overview of Ethnicity

In sociology, where "ethnicity" has been traditionally housed, ethnicity is viewed as a "set of sociocultural features that differentiate ethnic groups from one another" (Shibutani and Kwan 1965). In anthropology, Barth defines ethnicity around four basic elements: (1) a biologically self-perpetuating population; (2) a sharing of culture values and forms; (3) a field of communication and interaction; (4) a grouping that identifies itself and is identified by others as constituting a category different from other categories of the same order (Barth 1969:11).

Work produced within or closely adjacent to the concept of ethnicity is apparent since the time of Franz Boas. Although some of the studies are today regarded as limited, they are nonetheless, worth noting.

One of the initial works reflected Boas' concern with dispelling the notion of causal conections between race and culture and was written by Ruth Benedict (Race: Science and Politics 1974). Columbia University students, influenced by Boas, reflected his interests and

> "it is not surprising that the ethnographic research done by Columbia students during this period was largely done with American blacks, the focus of interethnic antagonism during the period" (Szwed 1979).

For example, Elsie Crew Parsons did folkloric and linguistic work with blacks in South Carolina, North Carolina, Virginia, Georgia, Florida, Maryland, Pennsylvania, and New York (Parsons 1923).

Other early endeavors in the field included Paul Radin's collection of former slaves' narratives (1969), Arthur Fauset's urban ethnography among blacks and his dissertation Black Gods of the Metropolis (1944), Hortense Powdermaker's Probing Our Prejudices (1941), and Gunnar Myrdal's An American Dilemma (1944). Myrdal's work was sponsored by the Carnegie Foundation of New York and included as project advisors Ruth Benedict, Franz Boas, Hortense Powdermaker, Melville J. Herskovits,

Ralph Linton, and M. F. Ashley-Montagu. Basically conceived as a study of American blacks, the project has been viewed both favorably and unfavorably, but significantly stands as a partial genesis of the evolutionary (sparse though it is) history of ethnic studies in anthropology.

Studies of racial groups were also evident-- from a variety of perspectives--among anthropologist. Obviously the above described study of blacks qualifies under this category, as does Boas' studies of Jewish people in his various essays on race, as well as Herskovits' attempt to define the term "Jewish." J. S. Slotkin's essay on Jewish intermarriage in Chicago spans both sociological and anthropological concerns, as does Mack Zborowski's "Cultural Components in Response to Pain" comparing the Jewish and Italian people in the United States.

As interesting as the above research proved to be, however, it was not based on a developed theory of ethnicity, but it does lay somewhat of a conceptual background for the genesis of anthropological ethnic studies. The turning point in anthropology came with the pivotal work of Fredrik Barth in Ethnic Groups and Boundaries (1969).

Following Barth's book (1969) and its subsequent impact on anthropology, research interest in this area was delineated at the spring meeting of the American Ethnological Society (AES 1973) and the IXth International Congress of Anthropological and Ethnological Sciences (1973). At the first,

> "the entire program of symposia was structured with a specific focus on problems relating to the investi- gation and comparative analysis of ethnicity and ethnic group relations" (Despres 1975),

and at the latter,

> "approximately two hundred of the more than twelves hundred contributed papers were organized in seven different sessions devoted to the discussion of comparative ethnic studies" (ibid. 1975).

In recent years, contributors to the literature include Barth (1969), constitution of ethnic groups

45

and the boundaries between them; Despres (1975), the competition for environmental resources to the processes of ethnicity; De Vos (1975), ethnicity at the deepest psychological level is a sense of survival through continuity in belonging, Cohen (1964), ethnicity is first and foremost situational; Hicks (1977), ethnicity as a tool employed primarily in the arena of social relations; Vincent (1974), the structuring of ethnicity; and others, such as Bennett, Moerman, and Kunstadter. With these contributions, and others following 1969, the increase in ethnic studies has gained such momentum that Leo A. Despres suggests that the study of ethnicity be designated B.B. (Before Barth) and A.B. (After Barth).

Barth's critical feature of ethnicity is self-ascription (not be equated with objective cultural criteria). To Barth, ethnicity is a continuing ascription which classifies a person in terms of one's most general and most inclusive identity (Barth 1969). Of great significance in this self-ascription is the maintenance of boundaries: boudaries (between ethnic groups) which exist in spite of contact and social interaction among groups.

Despres' Ethnicity and Resource Competition in Plural Societies acknowledges Barth as the leader in comparative ethnic studies. While critical of Barth's "extreme subjectivism" (Despres 1975), he contends that concepts and theories in the area of ethnicity have not far exceeded Barth's formulations.

Others, as mentioned above, have made contributions, also, in other areas of ethnicity theory. Despres is interested in the competition for environmental resources and the relationship to the processes of ethnicity. De Vos's perspective entails a psycho-cultural struggle comparable to nationalism or class affiliation. He perceives a sense of social belonging and ultimate loyalty necessitated by a basic sense of survival. Bennett's (1973) The New Ethnicity compiles the proceedings of the 1973 American Ethnological Society and included articles from Hicks, Despres, Neville, Willis, Jr., and others. Cohen's emphasis is related to the focus of ethnicity. Without exception, Cohen views ethnicity as first and foremost situational. Hicks, meanwhile, emphasizes social relations, while Vincent majors on the structuring of ethnicity: the extent to which the minority group is subjected to discrimination at the hands of the majority.

Most recently, Kunstadter (1978) has sought to delineate among "types of ethnicity." Using ethnicity as a generic notion, he distinguishes between two basic units--ethnic group and ethnic categories. He defines an ethnic group as a set of individuals with mutual interests based on shared understanding and common values. Ethnic categories is defined as classes of people based on real or presumed cultural features. These definitions are premised upon where and when the categorization is being made, and by whom.

In recent years then, anthropologists generally employ ethnicity as the

> "shift to multicultural, multiethnic interactive contexts in which attention is focused on an entity--the ethnic group-- which is marked by some degree of cultural and social commonality" (Cohen 1975:386).

The perceived characteristics of members may or may not coincide in the perception of members and non-members and the creation and maintenance of ethnic boundaries within which members operate is a major aspect of their own ethnicity.

Ethnicity and Identity

The development of self-identity, as a basic concept of self, "derives partly from the roles one assumes or is allowed to assume" (Hicks 1977:4). These roles, even when an aspect of a subjugated people, may become a source of security to the group's members. An increased level of cohesion among a group's members necessitates some form of mutual identification, and solidarity may well be achieved through the close alliance of ethnicity and identity.

Changes, however, are not unlikely in the identification process. If ethnic identification was simply a matter of birth, then fluidity would not be a paramount element of ethnicity. However, ethnicity is not static. It is constantly undergoing change and revision. These changes, where groups are concerned, may occur slowly or at a deliberately rapid pace. Often the changes in identity are the result of conscious modification of group behavior (Hororwitz 1975:114) either to narrow or widen the ethnic boudaries.

As changes occur some aspects of identification may be assimilated into another cultural unit. This assimilation may involve the unification of two or more groups to form a new unit (amalgamation), or it may involve the absorption of one unit by another (incorporation).

Regardless of the change or changes, the resultant end is a new or expanded set of ethnic boundaries designed to identify the ethnic groups.

> The critical focus of investigation from this point of view becomes the ethnic boundary that defines the group, not the cultural stuff that it encloses. The boundaries to which we must give our attention are, of course, social boundaries, though they may have territorial counterparts. If a group maintains its identity when members interact with others, this entails criteria for determining membership and ways of signaling membership and exclusion. Ethnic groups are not merely or necessarily based on the occupation of exclusive territories; and the different ways in which they are maintained, not only by a once-and-for-all recruitment but by continual expression and validation, need to be analysed.

> . . . The identification of another person as a fellow member of an ethnic group implies a sharing of criteria for evaluation and judgment. It thus entails the assumption that the two are fundamentally 'playing the same game,' and this means that there is between them a potential for diversification and expansion of their social relationship to cover eventually all different sectors and domains of activity. (Barth 1969:15)

For the Vietnamese in Oklahoma City, ethnic self-identity is an ongoing process vis-a-vis other Oklahoma City ethnic and cultural· units.

Variations in Ethnic Identity

The intensity of ethnic identification varies considerably in different social situations. It has already been noted that ethnic identification involves self-ascription and may not coincide with the identification given by persons outside the ethnic unit. However, even when agreement may occur, the self-identification process is a fluid one which changes as the societal context demands.

In Peoples: The Ethnic Dimension in Human Relations, Jerry Rose expresses the view that ethnicity

> is based on common ancestry deriving from race, religion or national origin. A closer examination of ethnic identity will show that, in a given society, one or more of these three criteria of ethnicity may be emphasized at the expense of the others. Sometimes...the three reinforce one another and provide a conception of peoplehood that is at once racial, religious, and national: 'White Anglo-Saxon Protestant,' for example, or 'Irish' which when applied to an American, implies not only his nationality but also his Catholic religion and white race. (Rose 1976:18)

It is also possible for two or more of these factors of ethnicity to function as excluding agents rather than including agents. For instance, the common identity of the Roman Catholic religion does not preclude persons from dividing along national lines. In the United States, Catholics identify themselves as Irish Catholic, Polish Catholic, or Vietnamese Catholic. Within the Baptist denomination a division may be based on factors of racial identification. There are Black Baptist, Mexican Baptist, and the mainstream of White Baptist.

Important, then, to the variations of ethnic identity, is the degree to which one emphasizes racial, religious, and/or national characteristics, and the context in which each characteristic takes prominence. These variations are present also within cultural groups, as well as between two cultural units. Variables within ethnic groups include generation, social class, economics, religion, and occupation.

Physical Features of Ethnic Identity

Physical features often are used as forms of ethnic identity because they are immediately apparent and are difficult to change. Height and body weight are often used a s general characteristics of an ethnic group even though they may result in stereotypes.

> . . . we value certain combinations of height, body shape, and movement and do not value others. In some systems, the combination of slenderness, delicacy of facial features and above-normal height spells breeding or aristocratic blood. Persons who have these attributes acquire power and respect in their own societies and are accorded the same by outsiders who have a similar view of the world. The opposite traits--a thick or heavy body, large and undefined facial features, and squatness--then become associated with a lack of power. Individuals of this type are not accorded respect, and are, in fact, ridiculed and made scapegoats. (Royce 1982:152)

Identity is also often marked by skin coloration. In the same way that preferences are developed concerning body size and shape, preferences are developed concerning skin color and the intensity of coloration.

During the colonial period, the degree of coloration played a prominent role in the determination of social status. It was generally conceived that lighter skin color indicated a higher status while darker skin color indicated a lower status. In the Philippines, for instance, the Spanish preference for light skin coloration became a factor of identification. The lighter the skin

the more closely one could be identified with the
colonial rulers (Rigal 1962; Isaacs 1975; Royce
1982). Later as nationalism began to sweep the
country, brown skin coloration was identified with
patriotism and independence.

In combination with these elements of physical
identification is the aspect of language. Language
is often a major aspect of ethnic identity for it
incorporates not only a physical reality, but an
emotional reality as well. For both the speaker and
the hearer, language evokes an aspect of identification, and is frequently employed by ethnic groups
as a strategy for maintaining and strengthening
ethnic identity.

Ethnic Adaptation and Identity

Ethnic identity is shaped and determined not
only by the group's personal preferences, but also
by what categories have meaning in the host society.
In ascertaining which strategies of ethnicity will
prove most advantageous, group profit is derived
from selecting strategies which are at least
minimally acceptable by the host society.

In Oklahoma City, a portion of the solid South
Bible Belt, a visibly prominent and most acceptable
category of the host society is its religious institutions. Therefore, as a strategy for adaptation,
the Vietnamese have employed their religions as
avenues of acceptability. As explained by Charles
Keyes concerning the Karen in Thailand,

> . . . considering the impact of Christi-
> anity upon the Karen. Although not all
> Karen in Burma are Christian, Burma Karen
> have come to be identified by many with
> Christianity. As in the case of the Chin
> on the west of Burma (cf. Lehman 1963), it
> is almost certain that the institution of
> the Church, in its international ramifica-
> tions, has provided for the Karen a basis
> for dealing advantageously with Brumans as
> institutional equals rather than as a
> benighted tribe. They, too, now 'have' a
> world religion.

Karen might just as well have become, and in fact are, Buddhist, but it is clear that their interests do not lie that way. For that way their choice is to try to acculturate to the Burmans, which would mean, given their relatively backward and remote habitat, being, predictably, poor Burmans and thus relative failures at the very levels of aspiration they would be adopting. In fact, it can be argued that one of the very reasons for an historical and continued Karen identity is that peoples in relatively poor areas are often better off in their own eyes if they maintain cultural styles and aspirations distinct from those of their richer neighbors. The answer in recent times seems to have been both to maintain their separateness and to identify with a modern social and religious system, that is, to identify with Christianity, even while not necessarily adopting Christianity whole-sale. (Keyes 1979:247-248)

Religion serves, then, as a means of "accept-able societal identification," and simultaneously, as a means of maintaining ethnic self-identity: particularly is this true in Oklahoma City for the various Vietnamese peoples.

CHAPTER V

STRATEGIES FOR ETHNICITY IN RELIGION

The Strategy of Religion

The religious traditions of Southeast Asia in general, and Vietnam, in particular, are very rich. Aspects of several religions have often been syncretised into an existing religion and contoured to the needs of a local village or societal unit. The major religions of the Southeast Asian geographical region--Buddhism, Taoism, Confucianism--are mutually receptive to one another (see Chapter 3). In addition, elements of Western philosophy and religion may be incorporated into these religions, as well.

As an area of identification, religion has proven to be advantageous from both the Vietnamese and American point of view. Many of the daily rituals and practices of the Vietnamese people are identified by the host culture as religious. Concurrent to that perception, religious tenets may offer a form of security during resettlement and a transitioning identity as the religion is adapted to the American community.

In assessing the adjustment needs of the Vietnamese in Oklahoma City, Dao The Xuong stated,

> Religion is an element of mental health (for the Vietnamese). Adjusting to a Bible belt culture from an Eastern philosophy is quite traumatic. Religions help the Vietnamese make the adjustment. (Indochinese Refugee Resettlement Seminar, October, 1980)

A Heterogeneous Population

The Vietnamese in Oklahoma City are not a homogeneous population. Their differences are reflective of variations in social class, religious traditions, geographical heritage, and political beliefs.

Vietnamese history has several predominant themes: (1) the resistance to outside domination; (2) the march to the South; (3) a sense of place; (4) the value of education; (5) the conflict between the divided North and South. Three of these factors--the resistance to outside dominance, the march to the South, and conflict between the North and South--are of particular importance to the Oklahoma City Vietnamese.

Resistance to outside domination accentuates the persistent maintenance of Vietnamese identity. At times they were conquered, but never dominated. For instance, although the Chinese occupied Vietnam for approximately one thousand years, (111 B.C. - 939 A.D.), the Vietnamese continued to maintain their own distinctiveness. As an older Vietnamese man recounted, "Some of the habits of the oppressors were sometimes adopted . . . we always stayed Vietnamese."

The march to the South highlights the plurality of Vietnam and refers to the nine hundred years of Vietnamese independence and the subsequent expansion from the Red River Valley in the north to the Mekong Delta in the south. Historically people identified themselves geographically from the upper, middle, or lower division of Vietnam, and today in Oklahoma City similar identifications are made of others, as well as of one's self. Significantly, the geographical identification bears personal characteristics as well.

> North Vietnam, the 'cradle of Vietnamese civilization,' has produced a type reputed to be overly ambitious, sometimes quarrelsome, and aggressive in all his pursuits. The Northerner supposedly is convinced of his intellectual superiority and is contemptuous of those from other regions, especially the easygoing Southerners. . .

> The man from central Vietnam is more attached to preserving the Confucian traditions of his land and the cultural heritage of his ancestors. It was in the center, in the lovely city of Hue, that the imperial court held sway, and there the emperors' tombs are still revered. The center is a proud land, where even peasant women wear their Sunday-best <u>ao</u> dai (the

Vietnamese women's national dress) to buy a
brace of ducks at the market. No one knows
what the men think. But it is known that
they like political power and prestige,
that they respect intellectual pursuits but
make poor businessmen. Life is hard in
central Vietnam, and austere, and Western
ways are slow to take hold.

The Southerner is a product of his environment: South Vietnam was long a frontier
region, settled by Vietnamese pioneers in a
'march South' that continued through the
nineteenth century. Land in the South is
fertile, and in peacetime life has tended
to be slower and easier than elsewhere in
Vietnam. The Southerner has a reputation--
perhaps because French economic and
cultural influence has been more dominant
in the South than in other regions--of
being more open to Western ideas, more
adaptable to progress, less rigid and
inhibited by traditional ways of doing
things. (Brown 1981:4-5)

The conflict between the North and the South
goes back to the sixteenth century with the civil
conflict between 1545 and 1592. In the twentieth
century, when the Geneva Agreement of 1954 divided
Vietnam into North Vietnam and South Vietnam, large
numbers of refugees fled south from the northern
communist government. Twenty-one years later, the
unification of Vietnam under the communist government
of the North precipitated another large refugee
exodus of Vietnamese people. These historical
displacements have created great suspicions among the
present day Vietnamese. It is not uncommon to hear
reports that a new arriving group of "boat people"
have been infiltrated by a communist agent, or that a
Vietnamese community member intends to undermine the
economic strength of another community resident.
This attitude is personified by the conversation of
a Vietnamese businessman:

Never go into a business with a Vietnamese.
He will take your business away. I would
have an American as a partner, but never a
Vietnamese.

Religion as Common Ground

Even though the intra-ethnic differences are many, one institution where common ground may be found is religion. This is, of course, not an absolute. Buddhists and Catholics are often ethnic competitors and there is, to be sure, status stratification within forms of organized religion. Nevertheless, Oklahoma City presently offers one Buddhist temple and one Catholic church as the predominant places of public worship. The exclusiveness of choice served to minimize fragmentation and maximize inclusiveness within the broader religious practices.

Religion as a Strategy for Revitalization

The role of religion in ethnic self-identity is, for some, the role of maintenance or revitalization of the traditional culture. Although this is not the primary strategy of the Vietnamese community at large, it is of importance to senior citizens within the Buddhist community. Attempting to resurrect traditional behavior which at times all but seems lost to many older persons, religion fills the primary role of reconnecting severed ties with the past. For instance, several Vietnamese parents have complained of their teenagers interest in cars and night life. This interest, they believe, has spawned a slow alienation from the family, and traditional Vietnamese values.

Following a Buddhist religious service, several women described their experience within the service as follows:

First Woman: To do this (worship as a Buddhist) is to be Vietnamese. The chants help me remember that I am Vietnamese of Vietnamese.

Second Woman: You cannot understand (to be) Buddhist for me. You may study with the monk and be a Buddhist someday, but that is hard (since) you cannot become Vietnamese.

Third Woman: More young people need to come (to
               the Buddhist service) so they will
               understand themselves (Vietnamese)
               better.

Although revitalization movements are best
depicted by Wallace and examples such as the Ghost
Dance, revitalization for these Vietnamese is not a
cooperatively structured group movement. It is
instead, a strategy, for reintroducing traditional
values to a portion of the ethnic community within
the host culture.

Religion as a Strategy to Obtain Material Needs

The Vietnamese, as a refugee people, were forced
to flee without the majority of their material
possessions. Although some of the refugees were able
to bring a portion of their monies or property, many
left with little or nothing. For that reason,
material needs such as shelter, food, clothing, and
living expenses became a matter of survival.

In order to meet this need, Vietnamese people
accepted the help of established churches and
charities, and some "converted" to the particular
belief system that was furnishing the assistance.
This conversion, however, often proved to be an
expression of gratitude or simply a strategy for
survival. Reverend Bob Lovejoy of the Department of
Cooperative Mission of the Baptist General Convention
of Oklahoma, explains,

> Most of our help (to the Vietnamese) is
> material. Things such as lodging, and jobs
> or help through our state's Friendship
> International groups . . . Most of the
> Vietnamese are Buddhists. Some have made a
> Christian profession of faith, but it's
> doubtful if true religious conversions have
> occurred.

Sister Anne Wisda of the Oklahoma City Catholic
Social Ministries (affiliated with the United States
Catholic Conference Migration and Refugee Services)
characterizes the Vietnamese as follows:

> There are a lot of successful people in the
> Vietnamese community with a strong drive to

succeed. Most are independent and aggressive in survival. . . . Buddhists hold on to their own beliefs. Catholics are dividing to the Baptists, Lutherans, and others who provide for them by giving them what they need. We have begun to require work in exchange for food and clothes. . . . The communities attach themselves to groups for material needs, even attending church for material benefits. They do not make attachments of affection and allegiances change in order to get more things . . . independent . . . me, myself, and I . . . successful today with no guarantee of loyalties for tomorrow.

Sister Marlosh of Oklahoma City Catholic Charities commented on this particular strategy, as well.

The pattern is persisting. . . . Refugees say they are Catholic, but the Baptist ministers offer food and they join the Baptist church. A lot of the Vietnamese people say they are Catholic, because they came through our agency, but not really. . . .

Religion as a Strategy for Intra-Ethnic Identity

The role of religion in Vietnam, and, thus, among the Vietnamese, is very complex. It has permeated every institution from the family to public political affairs. The village monk has historically exerted great influence and the support of local religious leaders has been a prerequisite for successful ventures in local hamlets.

The importance of religion increases when political characteristics are assigned to various belief systems. For instance, during the government of Diem in the south, Buddhists were generally considered to oppose the Diem rule, while Catholics were generally considered supportive. Competition already present between the two religious bodies heightened as demonstrations broke out in the streets of South Vietnam.

On the morning of May 8, 1963, there was a Buddha's birthday celebration in Hue. It was a peaceful celebration and the atmosphere was festive, though speakers did protest a government decree prohibiting the flying of the Buddhist religious flag. This seemed to them a special sign of intolerance since days earlier the streets of Hue had been decked with Catholic flags for the anniversary of Ngo Dinh Thuc's (Diem's brother) investiture as archbishop of Central Viet Nam. On the evening of May 8, an IVS English teacher at the boys' high school was on his way home from a coffee shop in the Citadel. Accompanied by one of his students, he crossed the main bridge across the Perfume River and immediately noticed a group of some five hundred people gathered around the Hue radio station. They were demonstrating, it turned out, because the government radio had refused to play any Buddhist music or otherwise acknowledge the holiday. . . . (Luce and Sommer 1969:114-115)

Ultimately, the Buddhists were credited, along with student groups, with toppling the Diem government. Although Diem fell as the result of a military coup, it is doubtful whether or not the military would have acted had public sentiment not reached such a fever pitch.

By 1965, the lines between the Buddhists and Catholics were tightly drawn. The Vietnamese society to some extent began to polarize around various factions of both groups, and the breach continued to widen.

. . . many Vietnamese, particularly Catholics, had dismissed the religious question as a divisive factor in Vietnamese life and politics prior to 1963, they now see it as another woeful stumbling block to national unity. Americans probably made more of the issue than Vietnamese, but government cabinets were chosen as much for religious balance in that period as they were for regional and other considerations. . . . In Hue the lines seemed especially sharply drawn. Catholic student leaders claimed that in the early part of the year, during the Buddhist demonstrations against the

Tran Van Huong government, they had been
pursued by Buddhist student leaders with
evil intentions. 'They tried to have us
kidnapped,' said one, 'and they are always
pouring recriminations upon us Catholics.'
(ibid. 1969:118-119).

The problems between the two main bodies and the
various groups within them vacillated in intensity
until the Struggle Movement of 1966. This movement,
a civil war within a war, was interpreted by many
American observers as basically anti-American. The
issues involved, however, were ones designed to
increase the working relationship between the South
Vietnamese government and the United States government through a series of definitive questions such
as, (1) how long did the United States plan to say in
Vietnam?, (2) what was the strength of the United
States forces within Vietnam?, (3) was the United
States presence designed to assist the struggle of
the Vietnamese people or further complicate it?,
(4) and who would be responsible for the behavior of
the American troops?

Seizing upon a prime opportunity, South Vietnamese Catholic leaders branded the Buddhists as
anti-American, and, therefore, communists for raising
such political questions. Americans interviewed on
television in the United States lashed out at the
perceived Vietnamese betrayal of American soldiers,
and demonstrations were held to demand the withdrawal
of American forces.

Some of the problems for which the Struggle
Movement people were asking solutions
seemed vague or minor to many Americans.
They were essentially political, economic,
and social problems, not religious ones.
The Buddhists were involved only because
they had taken up the nationalist banner.
'You must bear in mind that Buddhism in
Viet Nam is not the same as when it was
first born,' said Thich Tri Quang. 'Our
most sacred duty is to preserve our faith
and to advise our followers. . . . If our
country is lost, then our people would lose
their identity and Buddhism could no longer
survive. In other words, the Buddhists
must vigilantly protect their country's
interests, because that is in the interests
of their own faith.' (Smith 1968:81-82)

It was difficult for many outsiders to see in the minds of the Vietnamese Buddhist people the close identity between Buddhism, ethnicity, and nationalism; an identity which persists today. Consequently, there is a subtle yet pervasive attitude which at times denotes a stratified Vietnamese community predicated upon one's religious affiliation. The stratification varies depending upon which group is drawing the lines of demarcation.

Nevertheless, the feelings of competition continue to be present in Oklahoma City. In conversation with a Vietnamese woman concerning her religious beliefs, she said rather emphatically,

> I am a Buddhist because I am Vietnamese. All Vietnamese are Buddhist. Only those who are not all Vietnamese are something else.

The issue was most intense in October, 1981, when the Vietnamese Buddhist temple was closed by the City of Oklahoma for inadequate parking facilities. With a weekly attendance of 100-150 people, the attendance had grown beyond the parking capacity of the Buddhist temple.

Located in a residential community, the Buddhist participants parked on both sides of a narrow two lane street, hampering, but not completely blocking through traffic. When the neighborhood residents complained, a seldom used city ordinance was invoked to close the temple on the basis of failing to meet the city requirement of one parking space per each six members.

As attempts were made to re-open the Buddhist temple, frustration began to mount as the early efforts were unsuccessful. The delay was attributed directly to the Vietnamese Roman Catholic population. As a Vietnamese leader explained, "The problem would not exist if it had been Catholics. The Catholics would not have let it happen to them."

Another Vietnamese man accused a portion of the leadership in the Vietnamese American Association with complicity in keeping the temple closed. "The Catholic (Vietnamese) in the VAA are not supportive of Buddhist, either. They (will) not let the Vietnamese American Association help us."

A shop owner of the Catholic religion expressed her feelings in this manner: "The Buddhist temple is not my concern. I am a Catholic and I do not have anything to do with the Buddhists. . . . I do not know any from there (the Buddhist Temple)."

Even in the new society, the mutual feelings of competition and antagonism still run deep between the Vietnamese Buddhists and the Vietnamese Catholics.

Religion as a Strategy for Tolerance in the Host Community

Religion through the centuries has not been noted for its degree of tolerance toward others. A number of the most notable conflicts have been perpetuated on religious ground as various groups have claimed to contain the ultimate and exclusive "Truth."

In Oklahoma City, the Vietnamese Buddhists have, of necessity, developed a strategy of tolerance; a strategy designed to make themselves appear closer to the Bible belt mentality than they in fact may actually be.

The necessity of this strategy is apparent in the comments of residential Caucasian persons living in the same neighborhood where the Buddhist temple is located.

> Senior Citizen, Male: People here given them (Buddhists) lots of trouble. We don't like them practicing that funny religion.

> Mother of two elementary school aged children: The kids went down there (Buddhist temple) a couple of times until I knewed they were worshipping those statues. I don't want my kids around that stuff.

> Middle-Aged Male: There's some trouble down there (Buddhist temple), but I don't know what it is. Some of them were threatening to kill one of the monks. They made a real commotion. You know they can kill you with their feet. . . . damn scary.

Middle-Aged Married Couple, Female speaking: One of them we call Tony (the monks) because we can't pronounce his name. You know, his name ain't normal. It's real long. . . He teaches some of the children Kung Fu. The others though are strange. It's really kind of weird down there.

Senior Citizen, Female: Most of them drive better cars than me. Where do you think they get the money. . . . Do you think our government knows they're giving money to these people to go in there (Buddhist temple)?

Middle-Aged Woman: Yeal, this neighborhood has given them (Buddhist) lots of trouble. I say leave them alone. Maybe one day they'll be Americans.

In order to appear more "American," "Christian," and/or acceptable, the Buddhist have elected several strategies of accommodation. Although Buddhism normally places less emphasis on formal practices, organization, and membership than do the historical Christian churches, the Oklahoma City Buddhists give the appearance of a Christian mode.

Buddhists hold regular Sunday services at regular hours. Weekly services, on Sunday (a Christian day of worship) have not been a Vietnamese Buddhist tradition. A Sunday School is announced for children. Although it does not consists of a full hour of religious teaching as does the Christian Sunday school, the nomenclature is identical. Even the hours coincide. The Buddhist service begins at approximately 11 a.m.

Further identification in terminology involves references to various Buddhist branches or schools of thought as denominations. The temple is referred to as a church and is so listed in the phone directory. Often the monk is called a priest, not entirely non-Buddhist, and the Sunday morning service is publicly called a worship service.

Visual strategies include the arrangement of pews within the temple proper. The pews are approximately fifteen feet long and would make any Baptist or Methodist appear to be in familiar surroundings.

Notable, also, is the absence of shoes outside
the temple entrance. Reverent Buddhists would never
wear their outdoor footwear into the main temple
area. The "spectacle" of one hundred pairs of shoes,
however, outside the Buddhist "church" would only
accentuate the differences. To accommodate this
belief, the shoes are removed upon entering the
temple area, and placed inside the primary center out
of the sight of those outside.

Prior to entering the building, the Buddhists
stand prominently outside in the area most visible to
the residents adjacent to the temple location. The
"air" of a Baptist revival prevails as the Vietnamese, in very sociable fashion, embrace one another,
shake hands, wave to neighbors, talk boisterously,
and entertain the children. The festive mood is
reflective of a "Christian fellowship" and all the
evidence seems to point toward religious assimilation.

However, once inside, the atmosphere and the
service are distinctly Buddhist. People bow and
normally refrain from embracing. Incense is burned
and fruit is placed on the altar. The pews are moved
to the rear and people involved in the service sit
cross-legged on the floor. The Vietnamese literature
explicitly refers to "branches," "temples," and
normally, to "monks." The congregational participation consists of chanting and recitation, and the
climate is one of reverence and respect, as opposed
to the loud gathering prior to entrance. The
language for the service is always Vietnamese, even
though English has been spoken during the time of
greeting outside.

There is then, a change of form, but not a
change of substance. The teaching of martial arts to
neighborhood children, the appearance of Christian
similarities, and the change of terminology are all
accommodations to insure tolerance by the host
society. That is not to indicate that some changes
have not actually occurred. At a recent all-day
twenty-four hour feast and celebration, certain
"Americanisms" were obvious. Teenagers wore
bluejeans, and some of the elementary aged children
put ketchup on their egg rolls. Some teenagers
preferred hamburgers to rice, and talked about car
engines and American sports. Nevertheless, changes
in personal preference and style, notwithstanding,

matters of substance--doctrine, ritual, respect--have
not changed.

Religion as a Strategy for Identity Reinforcement

Religion is also employed as a strategy for
reinforcing existing ethnic-identity. The Vietnamese
Roman Catholics who worship at The Cathedral of Our
Lady of Perpetual Help maintain an identity vis-a-vis
Vietnamese Buddhists, as well as American Roman
Catholics.

This particular exclusive identity is not
readily apparent. Many in the Catholic congregation
dress in traditional Vietnamese fashion and the
service is conducted in the Vietnamese language.
Prior to the mass, the Vietnamese sing and chant
spontaneously in a similar manner to the Buddhist
ceremonial chants.

These identities, however, are also exclusions.
Vietnamese Buddhists do not kneel and genuflect prior
to being seated, nor do American Catholics chant
spontaneously prior to the formal mass. (This
chanting is not to be confused with prayerful
petitioning or glossalalia.) The language and dress
distinguish them from American Catholics, and
Christian rituals during the mass distinguish them
from Vietnamese Buddhists. In all phases of the
service, both structured and unstructured, there are
elements specifically designed to interrelate the
Vietnamese culture and the Catholic belief system.
Most signficant of all perhaps is the singing of the
equivalent of the Vietnamese National Anthem. The
song is sung when the priest makes his first
appearance, thereby interrelating the two primary
elements of the group identity: Vietnamese and
Catholic. Through these practices, the group is
identified with both Vietnamese and Catholics. At
the same time, the practices distinguish the group
from the two basic elements through selected
embellishments. In this manner, the particular
ethnic-identity and intra-identity of the group is
underscored and reinforced.

The observation that the service is employed to
reinforce existing identity is collaborated in two
conversations. The first is with Sister Marlosh of
the Oklahoma City Catholic Charities, while the

second is with Father Anthony Bao, the Vietnamese
Catholic priest.

> The Vietnamese Catholics are not identified
> with our culture (American culture). They
> have a separate way of seeing themselves.

> Catholicism is our (Vietnamese) faith. We
> are part of a universal frame and are
> easily adaptable. . . . . We are the same
> as American Catholics, but we are Vietnam-
> ese people. Through our Catholicism we are
> glad to share something of our Vietnamese
> culture. . . . We have no relationships
> with the Buddhists. We (are) just friends
> only.

Religion as a Strategy for Ethnic Cohesion

The Vietnamese people are traditionally xeno-
phobic. Close ties have existed between families and
village or community residents. To many the traditional values are fundamental to identity, and to
deviate from these values is a grave transgression.

Simultaneously, many Vietnamese desire to return
to their homeland. Their departure was hasty and
forced, and they view their presence in the United
States as temporary. However, the longer the
Vietnamese reside in America, the stronger the desire
on the part of the young to remain in the United
States. Father Bao explains,

> Many, especially the older people, fifty
> years and up or those who speak no English,
> would return if the communists were over-
> thrown. But many young people have good
> positions here (America) and do not want to
> go back.

This divided attitude concerns many of the
Vietnamese people who see this as a major step in
their children becoming "Americanized." Family
leaders have expressed concern over the Western dress
of the young people, the adoration for the American
automobile, and the general neglect of family values.
Perhaps this is reflective of a difference in adaptational strategies according to age stratification,
but however one analyzes the phenomenon, it remains
unacceptable to the community elders.

The question of reversing or impeding the process has arisen in several casual conversations. An example of the elder's concern came via the demands of the Vietnamese band which played for the Tet celebration in January, 1982. Upon acceptance of the invitation to perform at the celebration of the New Year, the band informed the organizers that they would play only if a color television were placed backstage for their viewing. The public celebration of Tet had been scheduled on the same day as the Superbowl game, and the youthful members of the band refused to miss the gridiron battle between the San Francisco Forty-Niners and the Cinncinnati Bengals.

To counter this Westernization, religion is being employed as a strategy for cohesion within the sphere of ethnic identity. Both the Vietnamese Buddhist and the Vietnamese Catholics are distinctly Vietnamese, and a renewed effort is being made to include the young people in these institutions. Youth programs, organizations, and especially designed teaching sessions have been organized for the community's young people. Pamphlets and booklets such as "Vietnamese Contributions to American Buddhism" are being dissiminated and a greater emphasis is placed on private devotional periods. The Buddhists, particularly, have scheduled weekend meetings, and once-a-month all day "festivals" aimed at emotionally and intellectually better incorporating the youth into the Vietnamese way of life. Also, both religions are placing a greater emphasis on youth participation within the corporate service.

Summary

As a foundational aspect of both Southeast Asia and the Bible Belt, religion is an ideal strategy for developing and maintaining ethnic identity. This identity is developing both inter-ethnically and intra-ethnically, as the Vietnamese community in Oklahoma City has stablized and continues to increase in numerical strength on a monthly basis.

CHAPTER VI

CONCLUSION

The Vietnamese of Oklahoma City are a refugee population who have become an economically stable, residential community of sizeable numerical strength. They are a population of perhaps twelve thousand or more and are growing steadily each month.

The support they have received from the community at large--economically and emotionally--has been a primary ingredient in the relocation process. They have concentrated on employment, housing, and transportation rather than medicaid and food stamps, and continue to develop greater self assurance about their role in the new society. Language acquisition continues to improve through English classes, and job promotions are viewed as a benefit of increased language skills.

With these and other characteristics of the Oklahoma City Vietnamese detailed in chapter two, it is possible to draw some preliminary conclusions. To be sure, the Vietnamese experience in America and Oklahoma is new (1975), but the hypotheses which follow bear investigation in the decades to come.

The Sooner Reception

The Vietnamese in Oklahoma City have basically been passively received allowing time for the generating of positive experiences with the host community.

Of course, arguments with the hypothesis may be made from both directions. It may be argued that the assistance of the religious community and the governmental organizations constitutes more than a passive reception. Conversely, the reaction of several local people to the Buddhist temple could be argued as the reflection of community hostility. Positively, the state government has assisted the Vietnamese through the government health programs. On the other hand, there are individuals who view the Vietnamese as being "too" different even in a time when more Americans are searching for ethnic roots and identities. It may also be argued that some assistance for the Vietnamese community has been predicated upon the guilt carried by some who view the Vietnamese as the residue of an immoral conflict. Still others approach the same dilemma from an alternate perspective claiming the Vietnamese presence simply keeps alive memories of an unpopular war.

These arguments not withstanding, the greater Oklahoma City community has simply allowed the Vietnamese to enter without a decidedly positive or negative response. The majority of the city has not assisted the Vietnamese people in resettling. Conversely, there have been no duplications of the anti-Vietnamese riots of Denver nor the backlash of hostilities displayed by the Klu Klux Klan in southern Texas. The people have been allowed to relocate without any strong demonstrative efforts on the part of the host community. This passive attitude of the general population has provided time for the Vietnamese people to turn the community sentiment in their favor through positive employment and community relations.

The Refugee Backlash

The Vietnamese refugee community of Oklahoma City has not encountered the harsh backlash of settlement that has been the experience of some of the other Vietnamese communities in the United States.

One of the primary reasons for this phenomenon is the educational and professional level of the Oklahoma City Vietnamese. Many Southeast Asian refugee people who have come to the United States are farmers or peasants and are often illiterate in their own language. They often do not speak English and are not acquainted with urban settings. Primarily from rural areas, the adjustment is not only to a new culture, but to a new and often confusing urban setting. The Vietnamese who have come to the United States have significant differences among them, particularly in terms of social standing, region of inhabitance, and religion.

The Oklahoma City Vietnamese are primarily well-educated urban-centered families. Many come from the Saigon Medical School or were prominent in the South Vietnamese government. Included within the community is an English teacher, a concert pianist, a professional artist, and high ranking military personnel. Several speak English fluently, and the Vietnamese American Associaiton conducts English language classes at all levels regardless of one's previous language acquisition.

In addition to the positive factor of language skills, the Oklahoma City Vietnamese population resides within an area where the number and availability of housing units is not a critical factor for the general population at large. In several other cities, Denver and San Francisco, for instance, the refugee community has settled in an urban area where housing is a major problem. It becomes not only a point of friction with the local community, but also with the other refugee or immigrant groups who simultaneously are competing for a limited number of dwellings.

In Denver, Colorado, Chicano people reacted negatively to the state's placement of twenty-four Southeast Asian families in a Chicano apartment complex. The complex already had a long waiting list of Chicanos. Violence erupted in the form of rock and bottle throwing, and isolated incidents of physical beatings occurred until the state removed the Asians from the housing unit.

In San Francisco, tensions have run high as well. Low income housing is at a premium and the Vietnamese presence has accentuated the problem.

> 'I came to San Francisco to find work, but before I get work, I need a place to live,' says Steven D. Early, a black construction worker from Little Rock, Arkansas. 'Only place I can afford to live is skid row. But now you can't get in there because of the Vietnamese. Can't find a cheap place any more because refugees have them all. Makes a man mad as hell.' (Chaze 1980:62)

Oklahoma City has adequate housing for the Vietnamese population without the addition of further strain on the existing population.

Job Competition

Another area of competition with the host community is that of jobs. The search for work in a time of nation-wide high unemployment holds the potential for increased conflict. Trouble has arisen in Gulf Coast areas of Texas and Mississippi where the competition for shrimp and fish is high. In Texas, the Klu Klux Klan has patrolled inlet areas looking for Vietnamese boats, and in Biloxi, Mississippi, a bumper sticker reads, "Save Your Shrimp Industry, Get Rid of Vietnamese" (Ardin 1981:387).

The resentment has at times fostered hostilities. In 1979, an American was shot to death. In 1980, several Vietnamese shrimpers had their shrimp boats torched by the local fishermen. Other clashes have resulted in injuries to parties on either side and the conflict is far from being resolved. As a student in junior standing at the University of Oklahoma, and a summer employee of a shrimping boat harbored in Rock Port, Texas, explained:

> The Vietnamese are taking all the shrimp
> and violating the areas reserved for long
> time fishermen. There aren't enough fish
> as it is. My captain said that Americans
> shouldn't have to give up their jobs or
> lower their income for some foreigners.

The state of Oklahoma, however, has one of the lowest unemployment figures within the entire United States for the first quarter of 1982. The job market is strong and the influx of refugee people has not threatened the job security of local residents. Moving slowly and methodically, the Vietnamese of Oklahoma City have been able to locate work for a large majority of their population.

Concurrently, the Oklahoma City VAA has been careful to acculturate the Vietnamese people in local job customs and practices. One difficulty on the Gulf Coast with Vietnamese fishermen involved the violation of the shrimper's routine behavior patterns. It was assumed that the Vietnamese understood the routines of the industry. Naive and uneducated in the Gulf Coast practices, the Vietnamese angered the shrimpers by bumping into their boats as they docked or by inadvertently making contact in the open waters. The hostile reactions to this contact was

72

not understood by the Vietnamese fishermen (Starr
1981:233). In Oklahoma City, careful attention is
given to the instruction of acceptable behavior
within a given job field or company. Local businessmen and industrial employers have been used to teach
small classes in regard to work protocol and
behavior.

The Vietnamese American Association

The Vietnamese American Association has been and
continues to be the key to Vietnamese adjustment.

The program the VAA provides has been fundamental in Vietnamese cultural survivability and
adjustment. As expressed in the discussion of job
competition, the VAA has been in the mainstream of
cultural education for the Vietnamese refugees.

The most recent assistance of Vietnamese as
sponsors for newly arrived Vietnamese refugees is
only one of a tremendous number of supportive
programs, both economically and emotionally. Serving
as a hub for the community process, the VAA has
helped to establish the Vietnamese population in
Oklahoma City.

Ethnicity

Ethnicity involves interaction.

The model of ethnicity is based on the interaction between the two cultural units. The
Vietnamese of Oklahoma are a group (groups) in
interaction with other groups within a common
geographical setting. They are not an isolated,
independent cultural unit, nor are they an assimilating unit in the traditional sense. They are
instead a distinct ethnic unit; that is, one that
employs factors of self-ascription in order to
maintain a separate identity vis-a-vis another
cultural or ethnic group.

Ethnicity and Religion

Ethnicity employs, but is different from, religion.

Ethnicity in the case of the Oklahoma City Vietnamese encompasses the totality of life of the ethnic
membership. Religion embraces a sizable segment of
the group's behavioral system, but does not encompass
the whole. There are, of course, examples where the
claims of religion have exercised a greater influence
over the individual than has ethnicity. Nevertheless, the specific case of the Oklahoma City Vietnamese exhibits a pattern of behavior and strategy
where ethnicity supercedes religion.

Religion and Ethnic Identity

Religion is employed as a strategy to maintain
ethnic self-identity while simultaneously acquiring
community acceptance.

Religion is employed as an aspect of inter-
ethnic and intra-ethnic self-identity (chapter five).
It has become a strategic tool in greater community
acceptability and intra-community identification. At
times employed interchangeably with ethnicity (i.e.,
to be Buddhist is to be Veitnamese), it serves as a
distinct strategy for adaptation.

Religion, then, become the bridge the Vietnamese
use to walk back and forth between the two contact
cultures. Rather than assimilating or acculturating
to the host culture, Vietnamese religion absorbs aspects of the contact culture without losing its own
identity. The bridge is employed in order to obtain
acceptability, but is never crossed with the intent
of permanent residence on the other side. Rather, it
is a catalyst to employ when necessitated by certain
social situations, but a return is always made to the
mother culture. It serves to gain acceptance while
maintaining ethnic distinctiveness.

Adaptation Not Assimilation

The primary strategy of the Oklahoma City Vietnamese in the employment of religion as an aspect of
ethnic identity is not assimilation, but adaptation;
adaptation in such a way as to positively increase
their present position while maintaining their ethnic
identity.

The goal of many Oklahoma City Vietnamese is to return to Vietnam. Consequently, the initial strategies of resettlement do not include acculturation. The goal instead is to adjust as adequately as possible to the newly encountered cultural environment, while simultaneously growing as strong as possible in order to facilitate a return with strength to Vietnam.

Should the goal to return not be achieved, the process of assimilation and acculturation still may not be enacted. The underlying assumption that following a given length of residence and exposure culture contact necessitates acculturation of one group to another has been demonstrated to be without foundation (Glazer and Moynihan 1963; Fishman 1966; Hicks and Kertzer 1974; Nagata 1974). Acculturation is not presently a desire of the Oklahoma City Vietnamese, nor of other numerically strong Vietnamese communities. As expressed in "Vietnamese immigrants and their adjustment to American Society," by Le Xuan Khoa in Dat Moi (New Land), a non-profit bilingual newspaper, "we can demand to be equal but we cannot and should not want to be alike" (April 20, 1981).

Summary

The entrance of the Vietnamese into the United States is still a relatively new phenomenon. In addition, the rate of entrance, more than 650,000 is seven years, has overwhelmed many assistance programs and retarded the opportunity to study scientifically the refugee phenomenon. Pressing needs such as food, shelter, education, language, and jobs have taken precedence.

The influx of refugees, however, has steadied as of 1982, and the opportunity for deeper observation and understanding has begun. Urban centers are draw-drawing large numbers of Vietnamese people, and population concentrations are accentuating the opportunities for interaction.

The strong and viable Vietnamese community in the urban center of Oklahoma City provides an excellent opportunity for learning about the Vietnamese culture and for examining the processes of adjustment. The conclusions drawn from such a study are as conclusive as is the community itself; a community which is continuing to re-define itself while developing a deeper sense of ethnic identity. It is still a new community, and as such does not need nor does it fashion concrete conclusions. It is, however, a dynamic, changing, growing community in which the traditionally held religions are employed in an ever increasing strategy to define and re-define ethnic self-identity in a society much different from the Vietnamese homeland.

BIBLIOGRAPHY

Aames, Jacqueline S., Ronald L. Aames, John Jung, and Edward Karabenick. <u>Indochinese Refugee Self-Sufficiency in California: A Survey and Analysis of the Vietnamese, Cambodians and Lao and the Agencies That Serve Them.</u> Report submitted to the State Department of Health, State of California, September 30, 1977.

Adler, Jerry. "The New Immigrants," <u>Newsweek</u>, July 7, 1980, pp. 26-31.

Alliband, Terry. "Quest for the Structure of the Sacred," <u>Reviews in Anthropology</u>, Spring, 1980.

Alland, Alexander, Jr. "Adaption," <u>Annual Review of Anthropology</u>, Vol. 4, 1975, pp. 59-73.

Almeida, M. Z. "Psychosocial and Psychopathological Aspects of Transplantation," <u>La Sante des Immigrants</u>. Comite Medical et Medico-social d'Aide aux Migrants. Paris: Societe d'Edition Droit et Liberte, 1972, pp. 105-128.

Anderson, Gerald H. <u>Asian Voices in Christian Theology</u>. New York: Orbis Books, 1976.

Arden, Harvey. "Troubled Odyssey of Vietnamese Fishermen," <u>National Geographic</u>, September, 1981, pp. 378-395.

Ashby, Philip H. <u>The Conflict of Religions</u>. New York: Charles Scribneis Sons, 1955.

Atkinson, Donald R., George Morten, and Derald Wing Sue. <u>Counseling American Minorities: A Cross-Cultural Perspective</u>. Dubuque, Iowa: Wm. C. Brown Publishers, 1979.

Aylesworth, Laurence S., Peter G. Ossorio, and Larry T. Osaki. "Stress and Mental Health Among Vietnamese in the United States," <u>Asian-Americans: Social and Psychological Perspectives</u>. Edited by R. Endo, S. Sue, and N. Wagner. Palo Alto, California: Basic Books, 1978.

Baird, W. David. <u>The Native American Experiences in Oklahoma</u>. Stillwater: Oklahoma State University Press, 1981.

Banton, Michael. Anthropological Approaches to the Study of Religion. New York: Frederick A. Praeger, 1966.

Barger, W. K. "Culture Change and Psychosocial Adjustment," American Ethnologist, Vol. 4, No. 3, August, 1977, pp. 471-496.

Barger, W. K., and Tham V. Truong. "Community Action Work Among the Vietnamese," Human Organization, Vol. 37, No. 1, Spring, 1978, pp. 95-100.

Barnes, Thomas J. Of All the 36 Alternatives: Indochinese Resettlement in America. U. S. Department of State, Senior Seminar in Foreign Policy, April 1977.

Barth, Fredrik. "On the Study of Social Change," American Anthropologist, Vol. 69, No. 6, December, 1967, pp. 661-669.

Barth, Fredrik, ed. Ethnic Groups and Boundaries: The Social Organization of Culture Differences. Oslo: Bergen, 1969.

Barzun, Jacques, Race, A Study in Superstition. New York: Harper Torchbooks, 1937.

Beach, Walter G. "Some Considerations in Regard to Race Segregation in California," Sociology and Social Research XVIII, March, 1934, pp. 340-350.

Bendix, Reinhard, and Seymour Martin Lipset. Class, Status, and Power: A Reader in Social Stratification. New York: Free Press, 1953.

Bennett, John W. The New Ethnicity: Perspectives From Ethnology. New York: West Publishing Company, 1975.

Bernard, William S. Refugees in Philadelphia: A Sample Study of Selected Aspects of Their Adjustment in a New Land. New York: American Immigration and Citizenship Conference, 1962.

Bernard, William S. Chinese Newcomers in the United States. New York: American Immigration and Citizenship Conference, 1964.

Bernard, William S. "Immigrants and Refugees: Their Similarities, Differences and Needs," _International Migration_, 1976.

Berreman, Gerald D. "Social Barriers: Caste, Class and Race in Cross-Cultural Perspective," _Papers in Anthropology_, Vol. 18, No. 2, Fall, 1977, pp. 217-242.

Berry, Brewton. _Race and Ethnic Relations_. Houghton Mifflin Company, 1958.

Berry, G. "Indochinese Refugees: Resettlement Progress," _Christian Century_ 93, October 27, 1976, pp. 931-933.

Berry, John W. "Acculturation as Varieties of Adaption--," _Acculturation: Theory, Models and Some New Findings_. Edited by Arnado Padilla. Westview Press, 1980.

Bloom, John. "A Delicate Balance," _Texas Monthly_, October, 1979.

Bohannan, Paul and Fred Plog, eds. _Beyond the Frontier, Social Process and Cultural Change_. American Museum Sourcebooks in Anthropology, The Natural History Press, 1967.

Boosey, Anne, and Others. _A Comparative Study of Relocated Vietnamese in Rural and Urban Arkansas_. Little Rock: Arkansas University, 1976.

Bosch, J. _Measurement of Acculturation Level With the Guttman Scale_. Unpublished Ph.D. dissertation from Stanford University, 1966.

Bradley, David G. _A Guide to the World's Religions_. New Jersey: Prentice-Hall, 1963.

Brantl, George, ed. _Catholicism_. New York: George Brazilleo Publishers, 1962.

Brohm, John. "Buddhism and Animism in a Burmese Village," _Journal of Asian Studies_, Vol. 22, 1963, pp. 155-168.

Broom, Leonard, and John Kitsuse. "The Validation of Acculturation: A Condition to Ethnic Assimilation," _American Anthropologist_, Vol. 57, No. 1, Part 1, 1955, pp. 44-48.

Brown, Donald N. _The Vietnamese-American Experience in Oklahoma_. Stillwater: Oklahoma State University, College of Arts and Sciences Extension, 1981.

Brown, Donald N. _The Urban Indian Experience in Oklahoma_. Stillwater: Oklahoma State University Press.

Brown, L. Dean. "Relief and Resettlement of Vietnamese and Cambodian Refugees," _Department of State Bulletin_ 72, June 2, 1975, pp. 741-745.

Bruner, Edward M. "Primary Group Experience and the Processes of Acculturation," _American Anthropologist_, Vol. 58, No. 4, August, 1956, pp. 604-623.

Burling, Robbins. _Hill Farms and Padi Fields: Life in Mainland Southeast Asia_. New Jersey: Prentice-Hall, Inc., 1965.

Buttinger, J. "The Ethnic Minorities in the Republic of Vietnam." _Problems of Freedom: South Vietnam Since Independence_. Wesley R. Fishel, ed. New York: Free Press, 1961.

Cadiers, Leopold M. "Vietnamese Ethnographic Papers," _Human Relations Area Files_, New Haven, 1953.

Cady, John F. _Southeast Asia: Its Historical Development_. New York: McGraw-Hill Book Company, 1964.

Cady, John F. _The History of Post-War Southeast Asia_. Athens, Ohio: Ohio University Press, 1974.

California Department of Social Services. _Indochinese Refugee Assistance Program: Characteristics Survey_. Sacramento, California: Statistical Services Bureau. Department of Social Services. Health and Welfare Agency, April 1980.

California Department of Social Services. _Refugees: The Challenge of the 80's_. Report of Hearings

Conducted by the California State Social Services Advisory Board. Sacramento: Health and Welfare Agency, Summer, 1980.

California Department of Social Services. The Assimilation and Acculturation of Indochinese Children into American Culture. Sacrmento: Department of Social Services. Health and Welfare Agency, August, 1980.

Cameron, Allan W., ed. Viet-Nam Crisis, A Documentary History, 1940-1956, Volume I. Ithaca: Cornell University Press, 1971.

Caron, Michael. Asians in South Louisiana: Filipinos, Chinese, and Vietnamese. 1980.

Carus, Paul, ed. Buddha, His Life and Teachings. New York: Peter Pauper Press, 1975.

Caudill, William. "Japanese-American Personality and Acculturation," Genetic Psychology Monographs, Vol. 45, 1952, pp. 3-102.

Caudill, William, and George de Vos. "Achievement, Culture and Personality: The Case of the Japanese Americans," American Anthropologist, Vol. 58, pp. 1102-1126.

Center for Applied Linguistics. Education in Vietnam: Fundamental Principles and Curricula. Arlington, Virginia: Center for Applied Linguistics, n.d.

Center for Applied Linguistics. On Assimilating Vietnamese and Cambodian Students into United States Schools. Arlington, Virginia: Center for Applied Linguistics, n.d.

Center for Applied Linguistics. On Keeping Lines of Communication with Indochinese Children Open. Arlington, Virginia: Center for Applied Linguistics, n.d.

Center for Applied Linguistics. A Personnel Resources Directory for the Education of Vietnamese Refugees. Arlington, Virginia: Center for Applied Linguistics, n.d.

Center for Applied Linguistics. A Selected Annotated
   Bibliography for Teaching English to Speakers of
   Vietnamese. Arlington, Virginia: Center for
   Applied Linguistics, n.d.

Center for Applied Linguistics. Vietnamese History,
   Literature and Folklore. Arlington, Virginia:
   Center for Applied Linguistics, n.d.

Center for Applied Linguistics. "Perspectives on a
   Cross-Cultural Problem: Getting to Know the
   Vietnamese," General Information Series, #13,
   Indochinese Refugee Education Guides.
   Arlington, Virginia: Center for Applied
   Linguistics, 1976.

Chakroff, Paul, and Louis L. Mitchell. New Economic
   and Social Opportunities for Americans and
   Indochinese on the Texas Gulf Coast. Washington
   D.C.: TransCentury Corporation, October, 1979.

Chan, Carole, Cambodians in America. California:
   Los Angeles County Commission on Human Rights,
   August 1975.

Chance, Norman A. "Acculturation, Self-Identification, and Personality Adjustment," American
   Anthropologist , Vol. 67, No. 2, April 1965,
   pp. 372-393.

Charley, S. R. "The Formation of Ethnic Groups,"
   Urban Ethnicity. Edited by Abner Cohen.
   London: Tavistock Publishing Company, 1974.

Chaze, William L. "Refugees, Stung by a Backlash,"
   U.S. News and World Report, October 13, 1980,
   pp. 60-63.

Chen, Jack. The Chinese of America. San Francisco:
   Harper and Row, 1980.

Ch'en, Kenneth K. S. Buddhism. Woodbury, New York:
   Barron's Publisher, 1968.

Cheng, David Te-Chao. Acculturation of the Chinese
   In the United States. Philadelphia: University
   of Pennsylvania, 1948.

Chu, Judy May. The Psychological Adjustment Process
   of the Vietnamese Refugees. Los Angeles: California School of Professional Psychology, 1979.

Chuyen Co Tich. _Popular Stories from Vietnam_. San Diego State University, 1980.

Citizens Applied Research Institute of George Mason University. _Proceedings of the First Annual Conference on Indochinese Refugees_. Held at George Mason University, October 24-25, 1979.

Clark, M. Margaret, Sharon Kaufman, and Robert C. Pierce. "Explorations of Acculturation: Toward a Model of Ethnic Identity," _Human Organization_, Vol. 35, No. 3, Fall, 1976, pp. 231-238.

Clarke, Susan. "Urban Ethnic Conflict: Selected Theoretical Approaches," _Urban Ethnic Conflict: A Comparative Perspective_. Edited by Clarke and Obler. University of North Carolina at Chapel Hill, 1976.

Caides, G. _The Indianized States of Southeast Asia_. Honolulu: University Press of Hawaii, 1971.

Caides, G. _The Making of South East Asia_. Berkeley: University of California Press, 1966.

Cohen, Abner. _Urban Ethnicity_. London: Tavistock Publications, 1974.

Cohen, Ronald. "Ethnicity: Problem and Focus In Anthropology," _Annual Review of Anthropology_, Vol. 7, 1978, pp. 379-402.

Cohon, J. Donald, Jr. "Psychological Adaptation and Dysfunction among Refugees," _International Migration Review_, Vol. 15, No. 1, Spring, 1981.

Conroy, Hilary, and T. Scott Miyakawa. _East Across the Pacific: Historical and Sociological Studies of Japanese Immigration and Assimilation_. Santa Barbara, California: Clio Press, 1972.

Conze, Edward. _Buddhism: Its Essence and Development_. New York: Harper and Row, 1959.

Coser, Lewis. _The Functions of Social Conflict_. Glencoe, Illinois: Free Press, 1956.

Coser, Lewis A. _Masters of Sociological Thought_. New York: Harper and Row, 1971.

Cotter, Barbara S., and Patrick R. Cotter. "American
    Attitudes toward Indochinese Refugees: the
    Influence of Region," Proceedings of the First
    Annual Conference on Indochinese Refugees.
    Compiled by G. Harry Stopp, Jr. and Nguyen Manh
    Hung. Fairfax, Virginia: George Mason
    University, October 1979.

Crawford, Ann. Customs and Culture of Vietnam.
    Rutland, Vermont, Tuttle, 1966.

David, Mrs. Rhys. Buddhism, Its Birth and Dispersal.
    London: Thornton Butterworth Ltd., 1934.

Davis, Stewart. "Classy Refugee Makes the Grades in
    Austin," Dallas Morning News, May 28, 1981.

Dean, Vera Micheles. The Nature of the Non-Western
    Non-Western World. New York: Mentor Books,
    1966.

Department of the Army. Minority Groups In North
    Vietnam. Washington, D.C.: U.S. Government
    Printing Office, 1972.

Despres, Leo A., ed. Ethnicity and Resource Competi-
    tion in Plural Societies. The Hague: Mouton
    Publishing, 1972.

Devereaux, George, and Edwin M. Loeb. "Antagonistic
    Acculturation," American Sociological Review,
    Vol. 8, 1943, pp. 133-147.

De Vos, George and Lola Romanucci-Ross, ed. Ethnic
    Identity: Cultural Continuity and Change. Palo
    Alto, California: Mayfield Publishing Company,
    1975.

De Vos, George. "Ethnic Pluralism, Conflict, and
    Accommodation," Ethnic Identity: Cultural
    Continuities and Change. Edited by De Vos and
    Romanucci-Ross. Palo Alto, California:
    Mayfield Publishing Company, 1975.

Dinnerstein, Leonard, and David Reimers. Ethnic
    Americans: A History of Immigration and
    Assimilation. New York: Dodd, Mead and
    Company, Incorporated, 1974.

Dinnerstein, Leonard, Roger Nichols, and David Reimers. Natives and Strangers: Ethnic Groups and the Building of America. New York: Oxford University Press, 1979.

Doan, Han T. Factors That Foster or Impede the Process of Acculturation of Vietnamese Refugees. Provo Utah: Brigham Young University, 1977.

Doornos, Martin R. "Some Conceptual Problems Concerning Ethnicity in Integration Analysis," Civilizations 22, Bruxelles, 1974.

Driedger, Leo. Religious Identity in a Plural Society: The Quest for Continuity in Diversity. Winnepeg: University of Manitoba, 1978.

Duiker, William J. The Rise of Nationalism in Vietnam, 1900-1941. Ithaca: Cornell University Press, 1976.

Dunn, Lynn P. Asian Americans: A Study Guide and Sourcebook. San Francisco, California: R. and E. Research Associates, 1975.

Durkheim, Emile. The Rules of Sociological Method. Chicago: University of Chiago Press, 1938 (originally 1895).

Enrlich, Paul R. The Race Bomb: Skin Color, Prejudice, and Intelligence. New York: Ballantine Books, 1977.

Ellis, Arthur A. The Assimilation and Acculturation of Indochinese Children Into American Culture. Department of Social Services, 1980.

Eliade, Mircea. Patterns in Comparative Religion. New York: New American Library, 1958.

Eliade, Mircea. From Primitives to Zen. New York: Harper and Row, 1967.

Eliade, Mircea. Man and the Sacred. New York: Harper and Row, 1974.

Eliade, Mircea. A History of Religious Ideas: From the Stone Age to the Eleusinian Mysteries. Chicago, Illinois: University of Chicago Press, 1978.

Elwood, Douglas J. _Asian Christian Theology: Emerging Themes_. Philadelphia: Westminster Press, 1980.

Ervin, Alexander. "A Review of the Acculturation Approach in Anthropology With Special Reference to Recent Change in Native Alaska," _Journal of Anthropological Research_, Vol. 36, No. 1, Spring, 1980, pp. 49-70.

Faires, Nora. "The Evaluation and Significance of Religious Diversity in an Immigrant Community." Paper presented at the Social Science History Association, November, 1980.

Fall, Bernard B. "The Political-Religious Sects of Viet-Nam," _Pacific Affairs_, Vol. XXVIII, pp. 235-253.

Fall, Bernard. _Hell in a Very Small Place, The Siege of Dien Bien Phu_. New York: J. B. Lippincott Company, 1967.

Feagin, Joe R. _Racial and Ethnic Relations_. New Jersey: Prentice-Hall, 1978.

Ferguson, John P., and Christina B. Johannsen. "Modern Buddhist Murals In Northern Thailand: A Study of Religious Symbols and Meaning," _American Ethnologist_, Vol. 3, No. 4, November, 1976, pp. 645-670.

Finman, Christine Robinson. "A Community Affair: Occupational Assimilation of Vietnamese Refugees," _Journal of Refugee Resettlement_, Vol. 1, No. 2, March, 1981. pp. 8-12.

Firth, Raymond. _Human Types: An Introduction to Social Anthropology_. New York: Mentor Books, 1958.

Fisher, C. _South East Asia: A Social, Economic, and Political Geography_. New York: Dutton, 1964.

FitzGerald, Frances. _Fire in the Lake, The Vietnamese and the Americans in Vietnam_. Boston: Little, Brown, and Company, 1972.

Fong, Stanley. "Assimilation and Changing Social Roles of Chinese Americans," _Journal of Social Issues_, Vol. 29, No. 2, 1973, pp. 115-127.

Foster, Brian L. "Ethnicity and Commerce," _American Ethnologist_, Vol. 1, No. 3, August 1974, pp. 437-448.

Fancis, Emerich K. _Interethnic Relations: An Essay in Sociological Theory._ New York: Elsevier Publishing Company, 1976.

Frazier , E. Franklin. _Race and Culture Contacts In the Modern World._ New York: Alfred A. Knopf, 1947.

Furlon, Elaine. "Asians In America," _Home Missions_, September-October, 1980, pp. 41-66.

Gaer, Joseph. _What the Great Religions Believe._ New York, New York: Dodd, Mead and Company, 1963.

Gans, H. G. "Ethnicity, Acculturation and Assimilation," forward to _Ethnic Identity and. . ._ Praeger, 1964.

Garbarino, Merwyn S. _Sociocultural Theory In Anthropology._ New York: Holt, Rinehart, and Winston, 1977.

Gard, Richard A. _Buddhism._ New York: George Braziller, 1962.

Geertz, Clifford. _The Interpretation of Cultures._ New York: Basic Books, Inc, 1973.

Geertz, Clifford. "Religion As a Cultural System," _Reader in Comparative Religion._ Edited by William A. Lessa and Evon Z. Vogt. New York: Harper and Row, pp. 78-89.

Gillin, John. "Acquired Drives in Culture Contact," _American Anthropologist_, Vol. 44, No. 4, Part 1, October-December, 1942, pp. 403-412.

Gim, Wever, and Tybel Litwin. _Indochinese Refugees in America: Profiles of Five Communities._ U. S. Department of State. Executive Seminar in National and International Affairs, April, 1980.

Girardet, Edward. "Refugee Crisis: Helping the World's Homeless." Reprinted from the _Christian Science Monitor_, December, 1980.

Glazer, Nathan, and Daniel P. Moynihan. Beyond the
    Melting Pot. Cambridge: Harvard University
    Press, 1963.

Glazer, Nathan, and Daniel Moynihan, eds. Ethnicity:
    Theory and Experience. Cambridge: Harvard
    University Press, 1975.

Gomez, Rudolph, ed. The Social Reality of Ethnic
    America. Lexington, Massachusetts: D. C. Heath
    and Company, 1974.

Gordon, Linda W., George S. Bridges, and Stephen A.
    Schroffel. "The Indochinese Refugees in
    America: New Ethnic Groups." Paper presented
    at the annual meetings of the American
    Statistical Association, Houston, Texas, August,
    1980.

Gordon, Milton M. Assimilation in American Life:
    The Role of Race, Religion, and National
    Origins. New York: Oxford University, 1964.

Gordon, Milton M. "Toward a General Theory of Racial
    and Ethnic Group Relations," Ethnicity. Edited
    by N. Glazer and D. P. Moynihan. Cambridge:
    Harvard University Press, 1975.

Graves, Nancy and Theodore Graves. "Adaptive Strate-
    gies In Urban Migration," Annual Review of
    Anthropology, Vol. 3, 1974, pp. 117-145.

Graeley, Andrew M. Ethnicity in the United States:
    A Preliminary Reconnaissance. New York: Wiley,
    1974.

Gremillion, Robert B. and Lyle Francis Hitzman.
    A Study of the Adjustment of Adult Vietnamese in
    the Baton Rouge Area. Master of Social Work
    Research Report, L.S.U., n.d.

Haaland, Gunnar. "Economic Determinants in Ethnic
    Processes," Ethnic Groups and Boundaries.
    Edited by Fredrik Barth. Boston: Little-Brown
    and Company, pp. 58-73.

Haines, David, Dorthy Rutherford, and Patrick Thomas.
    "Family and Community Among Vietnamese
    Refugees," International Migration Review,
    Vol. 15, No. 1, Spring, 1981.

Haines, David. "The Structuring of Kinship in Vietnam: Implications for Refugee Adaptation." Paper presented at the annual meetings of the Society for Applied Anthropology, Denver, Colorado, March, 1980.

Harris, Marvin. The Rise of Anthropological Theory. New York: Crowell Company, 1968.

Harris, Marvin. Cows, Pigs, Wars, and Witches: The Riddles of Culture. New York: Vintage Books, 1975.

Ha Ton Vinh. "Indochinese Mutual Assistance Associations," Journal of Refugee Resettlement, Vol. No. 1, November, 1980, pp. 49-52.

Hayes-Bautistia, David Emmett. Becoming Chicano: A "Dis-Assimilation" Theory of Transformation of Ethnic Identity. Ph.D. Dissertation, University of California, San Francisco, 1974.

Hearn, Robert M. Thai Government Programs in Refugee Relocation and Resettlement in Northern Thailand. Auburn, New York: Thailand Books, 1974.

Herskovits, Melville. "Some Comments on the Study of Cultural Contact," American Anthropologist, Vol. 43, No. 1, January-March, 1941, pp. 393-402.

Herskovits, Melville. Acculturation: The Study of Culture Cotact. Gloucester, Massachusetts: Peter Smith Publishing Company, 1958.

Hick, John H. Philosophy of Religion. New Jersey: Prentice-Hall, Inc., 1974.

Hickey, Gerald Cannon. Village in Vietnam. New Haven, Connecticut: Yale University Press, 1964.

Hickey, Gerald C. "Some Aspects of Hill Life in Vietnam," Southeast Asian Tribes, Minorities, and Nations. Edited by Peter Kunstadter. Princeton: Princeton University Press, 1965.

Hicks, George L., and Philip E. Leis. Ethnic Encounters: Identities and Contexts. North Scituate, Massachusetts: Duxbury Press, 1977.

Holtink, Harmannus. "Resource Competition, Monopoly, and Socio-racial Diversity," Ethnicity and Resource Competition in Plural Societies. Edited by Leo A. Despres. Paris: Mouton Publishers, 1975.

Hoover, Thomas. The Zen Experience. New York: New American Library, 1980.

Honigmann, John J. The Development of Anthropological Ideas. Homewood, Illinois: Dorsey Press, 1976.

Horinouchi, Isao. Americanized Buddhism: A Sociological Analysis of a Protestantized Japanese Religion. Unpublished dissertation, University of California, Davis, 1973.

Horn, Jack C. "Vietnamese Immigrants: Doing Poorly By Doing Well," Psychology Today, June, 1980, pp. 103-104.

Hsu, Francis L. K. The Challenge of the American Dream: The Chinese in the United States. California: Wadsworth Publishing Company, Inc., 1971.

Hundley, Norris, Jr., ed. The Asian American: The Historical Experience. Santa Barbara, California: Clio Books, 1976.

Ikeda, Daisaku. Buddhism, the First Millennium. Tokyo: Kodansha International, Ltd., 1977.

Indochinese Community Health and Education Project. Culture Shock: Picking Up the Pieces. Proceedings from the Region IX Mental Health Conference. San Diego, California, August, 1980.

Isaacs, Harold R. Idols of the Tribe: Group Identity and Political Change. New York: Harper and Row, 19745.

Johnson, Charles. The Path of Spiritual Progress in Theravada Buddhism. California Institute of Asian Studies, 1977.

Jackson, Joseph Peter. The Management of Projected Aggression by South Vietnamese Peole: A Study

of Acculturation. The University of Texas at
Austin, 1968.

Jeffries, Vincent, and H. Edward Ransford. Social
Stratification A Multiple Hierarchy Approach.
Boston: Allyn and Bacon, 1980.

Jones, Grant D. Symbolic Dramas of Ethnic Stratification: The Yucatecan Fiesta System on a
Colonial Frontier," Papers in Anthropology,
University of Oklahoma, Vol. 22, No. 1, Spring
1981.

Jones, James. Viet Journal. New York: Delacarte
Press, 1974.

Kalupahana, David J. Buddhist Philosophy: A Histor-
cal Analysis. Honolulu: University of Hawaii
Press, 1976.

Kelly, Gail Paradise. From Vietnam to America: A
Chronicle of the Vietnamese Immigration to the
United States. Boulder, Colorado: Westview
Press, 1977.

Kelly, Gail Paradise. "Adult Education for Viet-
namese Refugees: Commentary on Pluralism in
America," Journal of Ethnic Studies, Vol. 5,
Winter, 1978, pp. 55-64.

Keyes, Charles F., ed. Ethnic Adaptation and Iden-
tity, The Karen on the Thai Frontier with Burma.
Philadelphia: Institute for the Study of Human
Issues, 1979.

Keyes, Charles F., ed. Ethnic Change. Seattle:
University of Washington Press, 1981.

Khoa, Le Xuan, and John Vandeusen. "Social and
Cultural Customs: Their Contribution to
Resettlement," Journal of Refugee Resettlement,
Vol. 1, No. 2, March, 1981, pp. 48-52.

Khoa, Le Xuan. "Vietnamese Immigrants and Their
Adjustment to American Society," Dat Moi
Newspaper, Seattle, Washington, September, 1981.

Kim, Young Yun, and Perry M. Nicassio. Psychological, Social, and Cultural Adjustment of
Indochinese Refugees. Volume 4 of the Research

Project on Indochinese Refugees in the State of Illinois, Chicago: Travelers Aid Society of Metropolitan Chicago, February, 1980.

Kirsh, A. Thomas. Feasting and Social Oscillation: Religion and Society in Upland Southeast Asia. Data Paper Number 92. Ithaca, New York: Cornell University, Department of Asian Studies, July, 1973.

Kitano, Harry H. Japanses Americans: The Evaluation of a Subculture. Englewood Cliffs, New Jersey: Prentice Hall, Inc., 1976.

Koenig, Samuel. Sociology: An Introduction to the Science of Society. New York: Barnes and Noble, 1957.

Koranyi, Erwink. "Patterns of Acculturation in New Immigrants," Israel Annals of Psychiatry and Related Disciplines 11, 1973, pp. 129-133.

Kunstadter, P., ed. Southeast Asia Tribes, Minorities, and Nations, 2 volumes. Princeton: Princeton University Press, 1967.

Kunstadter, P. "Ethnic Group, Category and Identity: Karen in Northwestern Thailand," Ethnic Adaptation and Identity. Edited by Charles Keyes. Philadelphia: Institute for the Study of Human Issues, 1978.

Kunz, Egon F. "The Refugee in Flight: Kinetic Models and Forms of Displacement," International Migration Review, Vol. 7, Summer, 1973, pp. 125-146.

Landon, Kenneth Perry. Southeast Asia, Crossroad of Religions. Chicago: University of Chicago Press, 1949.

Latourette, Kenneth Scott. Introducing Buddhism. New York: Friendship Press, 1956.

LeBar, Frank M., Gerald C. Hickey, and John K. Musgrove. Ethnic Groups of Mainland Southeast Asia. New Haven: HRAF Press, 1964.

LeBar, Frank M. Ethnic Gruops of Insular Southeast Asia, Vol. 1. New Haven: HRAF Press, 1972.

Lee, Rose Hum. The Chinese In the United States of
     America. Hong Kong: Oxford University Press,
     1960.

Lehman, F. K. "Ethnic Categories in Burma and the
     Theory of Social Systems," Southeast Asian
     Tribes, Minorities, and Nations.   Edited by
     Peter Kunstadter.   Princeton: Princeton
     University Press, 1965.

Lehman, F. K. "Who Are the Karen, and If So, Why?
     Karen Ethnohistory and a Formal Theory of
     Ethnicity," Ethnic Adaptation and Identity.
     Edited by Charles F. Keyes.   Philadephia:
     Institute for the Study of Human Issues, 1979.

Leng, Lee Yong.   "Race, Language, and National Cohe-
     sion in Southeast Asia," Journal of Southeast
     Asian Studies, Vol. XI, No. 1, March, 1980,
     pp. 122-138.

Leslie, Charles, ed.   Anthropology of Folk Religion.
     New York, Vintage Books, 1960.

Lessa, William A., and Evon Z. Vogt. Reader In Com-
     parative Religion: An Anthropological Approach,
     fourth edition. New York: Harper and Row,
     1979.

Lester, Robert C.   Theravada Buddhism in Southeast
     Asia. Ann Arbor: University of Michigan Press,
     1973.

Levine, Gene N., and Darrel M. Montero.   "Socio-
     economic Mobility Among Three Generations of
     Japanese Americans," Journal of Social Issues,
     Vol. 29, 1973, pp. 33-48.

Levine, Gene, and Colbert Rhodes. The Japanese
     American Community, A Three-Generational Study.
     New York: Praeger Publishers, 1981.

Lewy, Guenter. America in Vietnam. New York:
     Oxford University Press, 1978.

Le Xuan Khoa. "Cultural Adjustment of Indochinese
     Refugees." Paper presented at the Seminar on
     "the Plight of Indochinese Refugees," sponsored
     by the Berks County Red Cross Community Service
     Council and the Conference of Agency Executives,

and organized by the Reading Area Community College. Pennsylvania: Penn State Unviersity, November, 1979.

Le Xuan Khoa. "Vietnamese Immigrants and their Adjustment to American Society." Paper presented at the Conference for IRAP Grantees and contractors, D.H.E.W. Region II. New Jersey: Brookdale Community College, April, 1979.

Lierberson, Stanley. "A Societal Theory of Race and Ethnic Relations," American Sociological Review, Vol. 26, 1961, pp. 102-190.

Lin, K. M., L. Tazuma, and M. Masuda. "Adaptational Problems of Vietnamese Refugees--Health and Mental Health Status," Archives of General Psychiatry, Vol. 36, No. 9, 1979, pp. 955-961.

Linton, Ralph, ed. Acculturation in Seven American Indian Tribes. D. Appleton-Century Company, Inc., 1940.

Liu, William T. "The Vietnamese in America: Perilous Flights, Uncertain Future," Bridge: An Asian American Perspective," Winter, 1977, pp. 42-50.

Liu, William T., and Alice K. Murata. "The Vietnamese in America. The Resettlement of the Refugees," Bridge: An Asian American Perspective 6, Winter, 1978, pp. 55-60.

Liu, William T., and Alice K. Murata. "The Vietmese in America: Refugees or Immigrants?" Bridge: An Asian American Perspective, Fall, 1977, pp. 31-39.

Liu, William T., and Elena S. H. Yu. Refugee Status and Alienation Theory: The Case of Vietnamese in U. S. Chicago, Illinois, 1978.

Liu, William T. "Vietnamese in America: Life in the Refugee Camps," Bridge: An Asian American Perspective, Spring, 1978, pp. 36-47.

Liu, William T. Transition to Nowhere: Vietnamese Refugees in America. Nashville: Charter House, 1979.

Llanes, Jose R. Moving Toward Cultural Pluralism, Part II: "Enculturation Within Group Culture-Cluters," 1980.

Locke, Alian, and Bernhard Stern, eds. When Peoples Meet: A Study in Race and Culture Contacts. Philadelphia: Hinds, Hayden, and Eldredge, Inc., 1946.

Lowie, Robert H. The History of Ethnological Theory. Berkeley, California: University of California Press, 1937.

Luce, Don, and John Sommer. "Defending the Interests of the Believers: Catholics, Buddhists, and the Struggle Movement," Vietnam: The Unheard Voices. Ithaca, New York: Cornell University Press, 1969, pp. 105-137.

Lyman, Stanford. The Asian in the West. Las Vegas, Nevada: Western Studies Center, University of Nevada System, 1970.

Lyman, Stanford. The Asian in North America. Santa Barbara, California: Clio Press, 1970.

Lyman, Stanford M. Chinese Americans. New York: Random House, 1974.

Mackie, J. A. C., ed. The Chinese in Indonesia. Honolulu: University Press of Hawaii, 1976.

Maclear, Michael. The Ten Thousand Day War, Vietnam: 1945-1975. New York: St. Martin's Press, 1981.

Malefijt, Annemarie de Wall. Religion and Culture. New York: Macmillan Company, 1968.

Malefijt, Annemarie de Wall. Images of Man, A History of Anthropological Thought. New York: Alfred A. Knopf, 1976.

Mandelbaum, David G. "Transcendental and Pragmatic Aspects of Religion," American Anthropologist, Vol. 68, 1966, pp. 1174-1191.

Martindale, Don. The Nature and Types of Sociological Theory. Boston: Houghton Mifflin Company, 1960.

Masuda, Minoru, Keh-Ming Lin, and Laurie Tazuma. "Adaptation Problems of Vietnamese Refugees: Life Changes and Perceptions of Life Events," <u>Archives of General Psychiatry</u>, Vol. 37, April, 1980, pp. 447-450.

McCarthy, John E. "Refugee Children from Southeast Asia," <u>Migration News</u>, Vol. 28, No. 2, 1979, pp. 3-6.

Mencarelli, James, and Steve Severin. <u>Protest: Red, Black, Brown Experience in America</u>. Grand Rapids, Michigan: William Eerdmans Publishing Company, 1975.

Middleton, John ed. <u>Gods and Rituals: Readings in Religious Beliefs and Practices</u>. University of Texas Press, 1967.

Mitchell, J .Clyde. "Perceptions of Ethnicity and Ethnic Behavior: An Empirical Exploration," <u>Urban Ethnicity</u>. London: Tavestock Publications, 1974.

Modell, John. "Japanese-Americans: Some Costs of Group Achievement," <u>Ethnic Conflict in California History</u>. Edited by Charles Wallenberg. Linnon-Brown, Inc. Publishers, 1970.

Moerman, Michael. "Ethnic Identification in a Complex Civilization: Who are the Lue?" <u>American Anthropologist</u>, Vol. 67, No. 5, Part 1, October, 1965, pp. 1215-1230.

Montero, Darrel. <u>Vietnamese Americans: Patterns of Resettlement and Socioeconomic Adaptation in the United States</u>. Boulder, Colorado: Westview Press, 1979.

Montero, Darrel. <u>Japanese Americans: Changing Patterns of Ethnic Affiliation Over Three Generations</u>. Boulder, Colorado: Westview Press, 1980.

Montero, Darrel. "Vietnamese Refugees in America: Toward a Theory of Spontaneous International Migration," <u>International Migration Review</u>, Vol. 13, 1979, pp. 624-648.

Mooney, Christopher. <u>Man Without Tears</u>. New York: Harper and Row, 1973.

Moore, John L. "Oriental Influence: Vietnamese Refugees Sink Roots in the U.S. Two Years After Arrival," Wall Street Journal, October 27, 1977, p. 1.

Murdock, George Peter, ed. Social Structure in Southeast Asia. Chicago: Quadrangle Books, 1960.

Murphy, Robert F. "Social Change and Acculturation," Transactions, New York Academy of Sciences, pp. 845-854.

Murphy, Robert F. "Religion," An Overture to Social Anthropology. Englewood Cliffs, New Jersey: Prentice-Hall, 1979.

Myrdal, Gunnar. An American Dilemma. New York: Harper and Row, 1944.

Nagata, Judith A. "What is a Malay? Situational Selection of Ethnic Identity in a Plural Society," American Ethnologist, Vol. 1, No. 1, March, 1974, pp. 331-350.

Nash, Manning. Anthropological Studies in Theravada Buddhism. Yale University Southeast Asia Studies, Cultural Report Series, No. 13, 1966.

New Orleans, City of. Impact Analysis of Indo-Chinese Resettlement in the New Orleans Metropolitan Area: A Task Force Report. New Orleans: Mayor's Office of Policy Planning, May, 1979.

Nguyen, Dinh-Hoa, ed. Some Aspects of Vietnamese Culture. Carbondale: Center for Vietnamese Studies, University of Southern Illinois, 1972.

Nguyen, Hy Quang. Perspectives on a Cross-Cultural Problem: Getting to Know the Vietnamese. Arlington, Virginia: Center for Applied Linguistics, 1975.

Nguyen, Quoc Tri. "Culture and Technical Assistance in Public Administration. A Study of What Can Be Tranferred from the United States to Vietnam." Unpublished doctoral dissertation, University of Southern California, 1970.

Noss, John B. _Living Religions_. Philadelphia: United Church Press, 1967.

Novak, Michael. _The Rise of the Unmeltable Ethnics_. Macmillan Company, 1971.

Oggeri, Lechi Tran. _The Unique Characteristics of the Vietnamese Culture That Affect the Process of Adjustment of Vietnamese Refugees to American Culture_. North Carolina State University at Raleigh, 1979.

Okura, K. Patrick. "Indochina Refugees: Mental Health Needs and Considerations." Paper presented at the annual meeting of the American Public Health Association, Detroit, Michigan, October, 1980.

Oliver, Victor L. _Caodai Spiritism: A Study of Religion In Vietnamese Society_. Leiden, Netherlands, E. J. Brill, 1976.

Olson, James Stuart. _The Ethnic Dimension in American History_. St. Martin's Press, 1979.

Opportunity Systems, Inc. _First Wave Report, Vietnam Resettlement Operational Feedback_. Washington, D.C.: Opportunity Systems, Inc., Contract No. HEW-100-76-0042, October 2, 1975.

Opportunity Systems, Inc. _Second Wave Report, Vietnam Resettlement Operational Feedback_. Washington, D.C.: Opportunity Systems, Inc., January, 1976.

Opportunity Systems, Inc. _Third Wave Report, Vietnam Resettlement Operational Feedback_. Washington, D.C.,: Opportunity Systems, Inc., September, 1976.

Opportunity Systems, Inc. _Fourth Wave Report, Vietnam Resettlement Operational Feedback_. Washington, D.C.: Opportunity Systems, Inc., September, 1977.

Opportunity Systems, Inc. _Fifth Wave Report, Vietnam Resettlement Operational Feedback_. Washington, D.C.: Opportunity Systems, Inc., October, 1977.

Padilla, Amado M., ed. Acculturation: Theory, Models, and Some New Findings. Boulder, Colorado: Westview Press, 1980.

Palmer, Howard. "Mosaic versus Melting Pot?: Immigration and Ethnicity in Canada and the United States," International Journal, Vol. 31, No. 3, Summer 1976.

Parrillo, Vincent. Strangers to These Shores: Race and Ethnic Relations in the United States. New York: Macmillan, 1980.

Parrinder, Geoffrey. The Faiths of Mankind. New York: Thomas Y. Crowell Company, 1964.

Parsons, John S. Americans and Vietnamese: A Comparison of Values in Two Cultures. Arlington, Virginia: Advanced Research Projects Agency, 1968.

Penner, L., and Tran Anh. A Comparison of American and Vietnamese Value System. Washington, D.C.: ERIC, 1976.

Perrucci, Robert, Dean Knudsen, and Russell Hamby. Sociology: Basic Structures and Processes. Dubuque, Iowa: Wm. C. Brown, 1977.

Pfanner, David E., and Jasper Ingersoll. "Theravada Buddhism and Village Economic Behavior," Journal of Asian Studies, Vol. 21, 1962, pp. 321-361.

Pfister-Amende, M. "Uprooting and Resettlement as a Sociological Problem," Uprooting and After. . . Edited by Ch. Zwingman and M. Pfister-Amende. Springer, New York, 1973.

Phung, Thi Hanh. "The Family in Vietnam and its Social Life," An Introduction to Indochinese History, Culture, Language and Life. Edited by John K. Whitmore. Ann Arbor: University of Michigan, Center for South and Southeast Asian Studies, 1979, pp. 77-84.

Poole, Peter A. "Thailand's Vietnamese Refugees: Can They be Assimilated?" Pacific Affairs, Vol. 40, 1968, pp. 324-332.

Poole, Peter A. The Vietnamese in Thailand: A Historical Perspective. Ithaca: Cornell

University Press, 1970. (Refugees from the French colonial regime in Thailand during the 50's and 60's.)

Popkin, Samuel L. The Rational Peasant, The Political Economy of Rural Society in Vietnam. Berkeley: University of California Press, 1979.

Powdermaker, Hortense. Probing Our Prejudices. New York: Harper, 1941.

Pruess, James B. "Merit and Misconduct: Venerating the Bo Tree at a Buddhist Shrine," American Ethnologist, Vol. 6, No. 2, May, 1979, pp. 261-273.

Purcell, Victor. The Chinese in Southeast Asia. New York: Oxford University Press, 1951.

Radcliffe-Brown, A. R. "Religion and Society," Structure and Function in Primitive Society. New York: Free Press, 1965 (originally 1945).

Ransford, H. Edward. Race and Class In American Society: Black, Chicano, Anglo. Cambridge, Massachusetts: Schenkman Publishing Company, 1977.

Ray, Nihar-Ranjan. An Introduction to the Study of Theravada Buddhism in Burma. Calcutta: Calcutta University Press, 1946.

Razas, Wade, and Vincent Maruggi. "Vietnamese Refugee Living Conditions In the New Orleans Metro Area." Division of Business and Economic Research, University of New Orleans, November 1978.

Redfield, Robert. "Culture Contact in Central America." When Peoples Meet: A Study in Race and Culture Contacts. Edited by Alain Locke. Philadelphia: Hinds, Haydn, and Eldridge, Inc., 1946.

Redfield, Robert, Ralph Linton, and Melville Herskovits. "Memorandum for the Study of Acculturation," American Anthropologist, Vol. 38, 1936, pp. 220-234.

Review Articles. "What Directions for Race/Ethnic Relations? A Kaleidoscope of Options," American Anthropologist, June, 1979, pp. 320-324.

Richardson, A. "A Theory and Method for the Psychological Study of Assimilation," International Migration Review 2, 1967, pp. 3-29.

Rogg, Eleanor Meyer. The Assimilation of Cuban Exiles: The Role of Community and Class. New York: Aberdeen Press, 1974.

Rohrs, Richard C. The German-American Experience in Oklahoma. Stillwater: Oklahoma State University, 1981.

Rose, Jerry D. Peoples: The Ethnic Dimension in Human Relations. Chicago: Rand McNally, 1976.

Rose, Peter I. They and We: Racial and Ethnic Relations in the United States. Random House, 1974.

Ross, Val. "Afloat in the New Land," Maclean's, October 27, 1980, pp. 50-60.

Royce, Anya Peterson. Ethnic Identity. Bloomington, Indiana: Indiana University Press, 1982.

Rubin, Gary. "The Process of Immigrant Acculturation: Recent Findings and Policy Implications," Migration Today, Vol. 8, No. 3, 1980, pp. 19-22.

Rutledge, Paul. "The Vietnamese-Americans of Oklahoma City," The Vietnam Forum, Yale University,, Journal of Southeast Asian Studies, Summer-Fall, 1983, no. 2.

Rutledge, Paul. "The Vietnamese Transition through Kailua, Hawaii: A Personal and Historical Perspective," East Asia Journal of Theology, Oct. 1983, vol. 1, no. 2.

Rutledge, Paul. "Buddhism Among Overseas Vietnamese." Unpublished paper presented at the Association for Asian Studies, April, 1982.

Ruff, Gunther Hermann. "The Impact of Refugees of the West German Economy: A Study in Refugee Integration." Harvard University, 1978.

Sangharakshita, Bhikshu. A Survey of Buddhism. Boulder, Colorado: Shambhala Publishers, 1980.

Sarwer Foner, G. J., J. Gellert, and E. K. Koranyi. "The Immigrant Acculturation Scale: A Socio-Psychiatric Tool for Assessing Immigrant Adaptation," _Laval Med_. 41, No. 4, 1970, pp. 465-477.

Schaefer, Richard T. _Racial and Ethnic Groups_. Boston: Little, Brown, and Company, 1979.

Schecter, Jerrold. _The New Face of Buddha_. New York: Coward, McCann and Geohegan, 1967.

Schedler, Norbert O. _Philosophy of Religion: Contemporary Perspectives_. New York: Macmillan Publishing Company, 1974.

Schermerhorn, Richard A. _Comparative Ethnic Relations: A Framework for Theory and Research_. New York: Random House, 1970.

Scott, George M., Jr. "The Hmong Refugees of San Diego: Initial Strategies of Adjustment," _Proceedings of the First Annual Conference on Indochinese Refugees_. Compiled by G. Harry Stopp, Jr. and Nguyen Manh Hung. Fairfax, Virginia: George Mason Unviersity, October, 1979.

Seller, Maxine. _To Seek America: A History of Ethnic Life in the United States_. Jerome Ozer, Publisher, Inc., 1977.

Shannon, Lyle W. "The Place of Intergroup Relations in Scientific Sociology," _Reviews in Anthropology_, Spring, 1981, pp. 141-146.

Shibutani, Tamotsu, and Kian M. Kwan. _Ethnic Stratification: A Comparative Approach_. New York: Macmillan Company, 1964.

Siegel, Bernard J., ed. _Acculturation, Critical Abstracts, North America_. Stanford Anthropological Series, Stanford University Press, 1955.

Simon, Rita J. "Refugee Families' Adjustment and Aspirations: A Comparison of Soviet Jewish and Vietnamese Immigrants." Unpublished paper, University of Illinois, January, 1981.

Simon, Walter B. Cultural Identity Between Assimila-
    tion and Tradition. Soziologisches Institute,
    University Wien, Austria, 1978.

Simpson, George, and J. Milton Yinger. Racial and
    Cultural Minorities. New York: Harper and Row,
    1965.

Skinner, G. William. The Thailand Chinese: Assimi-
    lation in a Changing Society. New York: Asia
    Society, 1963.

Skinner, Kenneth A., and Glenn L. Hendricks. "The
    Shaping of Ethnic Self-Identity Among Indo-
    chinese Refugees," Journal of Ethnic Studies,
    Vol. 7, No. 3, Fall, 1979, pp. 25-42.

Sin, Francis Lan Hui, and John A. Rubio. "The Social
    Problems of the Vietnamese on Public Assistance
    in Salt Lake County." Graduate School of Social
    Work, University of Utah, Spring, 1980.

Smallwood, James M. The Black Experience in Okla-
    homa. Stillwater: Oklahoma State University,
    1981.

Smith, Heeston. The Religions of Man. New York:
    Mentor Books, 1958.

Smith, Michael M. The Mexican-American Experience in
    Oklahoma. Stillwater: Oklahoma State Univer-
    sity, 1981.

Smith, Ralph. "Religion," Vietnam and the West.
    Ithaca: New York: Cornell University Press,
    1971.

Smith, R. B. "The Cycle of Confucianization in Viet-
    nam," Aspects of Vietnamese History. Honolulu:
    University Press of Hawaii, 1973, pp. 1-29.

Smither, Robert. "Psychological Study of Refugee
    Acculturation: A Review of the Literature,"
    Journal of Refugee Resettlement, Vol. 1, No. 2,
    March, 1981, pp. 58-62.

Soberano, Rawlein. "The Vietnamese of New Orleans:
    Problems of America's Newest Immigrants." New
    Orleans: Educational Resources, 1978.

Spencer, Robert F.   Japanese Buddhism in the United
    States, 1940-1945: A. Study in Acculturation.
    University of California, Berkeley, 1947.

Spencer, Robert F., ed. Religion and Change in
    Contemporary Asia. Minneapolis: University of
    Minnesota Press, 1971.

Spencer, Sidney. Mysticism in World Religion. New
    York: A. S. Barnes and Co., 1963.

Spiro, Melford E.   "The Acculturation of American
    Ethnic Groups," American Anthropologist, Vol.
    57, No. 6, Part I, December, 1955, pp.
    1240-1252.

Spiro, Melford, and Roy D'Andrade. "A Cross-Cultural
    Study of Some Supernational Beliefs," American
    Anthropologist, Vol. 60, pp. 456-466.

Spiro, Melford E. Burmese Supernaturalism. Phila-
    delphia: Institute for the Study of the Human
    Issues, 1967.

Stanford, Lyman. The Asian in the West. Reno, 1971.

Starkes, M. Thomas. Today's World Religions. New
    Orleans: Louisiana: Insight Press, 1978.

Starr, P. D.   Adaptation and Stress Among Vietnamese
    Refugees. Auburn, Alabama: Department of
    Sociology and Anthropology, 1980.

Starr, Paul, and Alden Roberts. "Community Structure
    and Vietnamese Refugee Adaptation: The Signifi-
    cance of Context." From the American Socio-
    logical Association Meeting, New York, 1980.

Starr, Paul D. "Troubled Waters: Vietnamese Fisher-
    folk on American's Gulf Coast," International
    Migration Review, Spring-Summer, 1981, pp.
    226-238.

Starr, Paul D. "Vietnamese Fisherfolk on the Gulf
    Coast: A Case Study of Local Reactions to
    Refugee Resettlement." Revised version of paper
    presented at the annual meetings of the Society
    for Applied Anthropology, Denver, Colorado,
    March 20, 1980.

Steele, C. Hay. The New Ethnicity: Perspectives From Ethnology. New York: West Publishing Company, 1975, pp. 167-178.

Stein, Barry N. "The Refugee Experience: An Overview of Refugee Research." Paper presented at a conference on the Refugee Experience sponsored by the Royal Anthropological Institute and the Minority Rights Group. London, England, February, 1980.

Stein, Howard F., and Robert F. Hill. The Ethnic Imperative. University Park: Pennsylvania State University Press, 1977.

Steinfield, Melvin. Cracks in the Melting Pot: Racism and Discrimination in American History. Beverly Hills: Glencoe Press, 1970.

Stern, Lewis M. "The Vietnamese Explusion of the Chinese Residents: Perceptions and Memories of the Vietnamese Hoa." Annual meeting of the Association for Asian Studies, March 13-15, 1981, pp. 1-15.

Stern, T. "Ariya and the Golden Buddha: A Millenarian Buddhist Sect Among the Karen," Journal of Asian Studies, Vol. 27, 1968, pp. 297-328.

Stone, John ed. Race, Ethnicity, and Social Change. North Scituate: Duxbury Press, 1977.

Snug, Betty L. Mountain of Gold: The Story of the Chinese in America. New York: Macmillan and Company, 1967.

Swearer, Donald K. Buddhism in Transition. Philadelphia: Westminster Press, 1970.

Swearer, Donald K. Buddhism. Niles, Illinois: Argus Communications, 1977.

Szwed, John. "The Ethnography of Ethnic Groups in the United States, 1920-1950," The Uses of Anthropology. Edited by Walter Goldschmidt. Published by AAA, 1979, pp. 100-109.

Takakusu, J. The Essentials of Buddhist Philosophy. Honolulu: University of Hawaii Press, 1936.

Taniwaki, Marge Yamada, et al. "Denver's Westside Community: The Impact of Indochinese Resettlement on a Predominantly Chicano Neighborhood," Proceedings of the First Annual Conference on Indochinese Refugees. Compiled by G. Harry Stopp, Jr. and Nguyen Manh Hung. Fairfax, Virginia: George Mason University, October, 1979.

Tepper, Elliot L., ed. Southeast Asian Exodus: From Tradition to Resettlement, Understanding Refugees from Laos, Kampuchea, and Vietnam in Canada. Ottawa: The Canadian Asian Studies Association, 1980.

Teske, R. H., and B. H. Nelson. "Acculturation and Assimilation: A Classification," American Ethnologist 1, 1974, pp. 351-367.

The Daily Oklahoman. "Viet Fishermen's Suit Seeks Protection from Klan." April 17, 1981.

Thomas, Patrick. "French and United States Policy and Indochinese Refugees." Paper presented at the annual meetings of the American Anthropological Association, Washington, D.C., December, 1980.

Thompson, Stephen I. "Religion Conversion and Religious Zeal in an Overseas Enclave: The Case of the Japanese in Bolivia," Anthropological Quarterly, Vol. 41, No. 4, October, 1968.

Thompson, Stephen I. "Survival of Ethnicity in the Japanese Community of Lima, Peru," Urban Anthropology, Vol. 3, No. 2, 1974, pp. 243-261.

Thompson, Stephen I. "East Asians in Peru: Middleman Minorities?" Transactions of the 1976 Annual Meeting, Southwest Conference on Asian Studies, II, 1977, pp. 159-167.

Thompson, Stephen I. "Separate but Superior: Japanese in Bolivia," Ethnic Encounter: Identities and Contexts. Edited by George L. Hicks and Philip E. Leis. North Scituate: Duxbury Press, 1977, pp. 89-101.

Thompson, Stephen I. "Assimilation and Nonassimilation of Asian Americans and Asian Peruvians," Comparative STudies in Society and History, Vol. 21, 1979, pp. 572-588.

Thurnwald, Richard. "The Psychology of Acculturation," American Anthropologist, Vol. 34, 1932,
pp. 557-569.

Thuy, Vuong G. Getting to Know the Vietnamese and
Their Culture. New York: Frederick Ungar
Publishing Company, 1976.

Tinker, John M. "Intermarriage and Ethnic Boundaries: The Japanese American Case," Journal of
Social Issues 29, 1973, pp. 49-66.

Tran Tuong Nhu. "Vietnam Refugees: The Trauma of
Exile," U.S. Commission on Civil Rights, Civil
Rights Digest Vol. 9, No. 1, Fall, 1976, pp.
59-62.

Tran Van Mai. "Cross Cultural Understanding and Its
Implications in Counseling," printed in
"Indochinese Health Care." A Conference for
Health Professionals, San Diego, California,
November 27, 1979.

United Nations High Commission for Refugees. Collection of International Instruments Concerning
Refugees. Geneva, Switzerland: UNHCR, 1979.

United Nations Intergovernmental Committee for Migra-
tion. "Adaptation and Integration of Permanent
Immigrants." Paper presented at the Fifth
Seminar on Adaptation and Integration of
Permanent Immigrants, Geneva, Switzerland, 1981,
pp. 1-23.

U. S. Commission on Civil Rights. Success of Asian
Americans: Face or Fiction? Washington, D.C.:
U.S. Government Printing Office, September,
1980.

United States Committee for Refugee, Inc. 1980 World
Refugee Survey. New York, N.Y.: United States
Committee for Refugees, Inc., 1980.

U. S. Congress. House of Representatives. Committee
on the Judiciary. Subcommittee on Immigration,
Citizenship and International Law. Evacuation
from South Vietnam, Migration and Refugee Assistance Act of 1962. 94th Congress, 1st Session,
April 9, 1975.

U.S. Congress. House of Representatives. Committee on the Judiciary. Subcommittee on Immigration, Refugees, and International Law. Refugee Act of 1979: Hearings before the Subcommittee on Immigration, Refugees, and International Law. 96th Congress, 1st Session. Washington, D.C., May, 1979.

U.S. Congress. Senate. Committee on the Judiciary. "Refugees and Civil War Casualty Problems in Laos and Cambodia," Hearing before the Subcommittee to Investigate Problems Connected with Refugees and Escapees, 91st Congress, 2nd Session. Washington, D.C.: Government Printing Office, May 7, 1970.

U.S. Congress. Senate. Committee on the Judiciary. Subcommittee on Refugees and Escapees. Aftermath of War: Humanitarian Problems of Southeast Asia. 94th Congress, 2nd Session. Washington, D.C.: Government Printing Office, May 17, 1976.

U.S. Congress. Senate. Committee on the Judiciary. Subcommittee to Investigate Problems Connected with Refugees and Escapees. Aftermath of War: Humanitarian Problems of Southeast Asia: Staff Report. 94th Congress, 2nd Session. Washington, D.C: Government Printing Office, May 27, 1976.

U.S. Congress. Senate. Committee on the Judiciary. "Refugee and Humanitarian Problems in Vietnam," Hearing before the Committee on the Judiciary, 95th Congress, 2nd Session. Washington, D.C.: Government Printing Office, August 22, 1978.

U.S. Department of Health, Education, and Welfare. HEW Refugee Task Force. Report to the Congress. Washington, D.C.: U.S. DHEW, March 15, 1976.

U.S. Department of Health, Education, and Welfare. HEW Refugee Task Force. Report to the Congress. Washington, D.C.: U.S. DHEW, June 15, 1976.

U.S. Department of Health, Education, and Welfare. HEW REfugee Task Force. Report to the Congress. Washington, D.C.: U.S. DHEW, September 20, 1976.

U.S. Department of Health, Education, and Welfare. HEW Refugee Task Force. Report to the Congress. Washington, D.C.: U.S. DHEW, December 20, 1976.

U.S. Department of Health, Education, and Welfare. HEW Refugee Task Force. Report to the Congress. Washington, D.C.: U.S. DHEW, March 21, 1977.

U.S. Department of Health, Education, and Welfare. HEW Refugee Task Force. Report to the Congress. Washington, D.C.: U.S. DHEW, June 20, 1977.

U.S. Department of Health, Education, and Welfare. HEW Refugee Task Force. Report to the Congress. Washington, D.C.: U.S. DHEW, September 21, 1977.

U.S. Department of Health, Education, and Welfare. HEW Refugee Task Force. Report to the Congress. Washington, D.C.: U.S. DHEW, December 31, 1977.

U.S. Department of State. "Refugee Fact Sheet: Indochinese Resettlement in the United States." Special Report Number 68, February, 1980.

U.S. General Accounting Office. The Indochinese Exodus: A Humanitarian Dilemma: Report to the Congress. By the Comptroller General of the United States. Washington, D.C., April 24, 1979.

U.S. Bureau of Naval Personnel. Vietnamese Time Concepts and Behavior. Sai-Gon, 1968.

Van Den Berghe. Race and Ethnicity. New York: Basic Books, 1970.

Van Deusen, John, Cynthia Coleman, and others. "Southeast Asian Social and Cultural Customs: Similarities and Differences. Part 1," Journal of Refugee Resettlement, Vol. 1, No. 1, November, 1980, pp. 20-39.

Vietnamese American Association. "Adjustment of the Vietnamese Refugee to the New Environment." 1980 Spring Survey. VAA, Mental Health Projects, 1980.

Vietnamese American Association. "American-Vietnamese Cross-Cultural Information." n.d.

Vietnamese Buddhist Temple. The Presence of Vietnamese Buddhists in America. Los Angeles, California: Vietnamese Buddhist Temple, 1981.

Vincent, Joan. "The Structuring of Ethnicity," <u>Human Organization</u>, Vol. 33,. No. 4, Winter, 1974, pp. 375-379.

Vos, Howard F. <u>Religions in a Changing World</u>. Chicago, Illinois: Moody Press, 1967.

Waley, Arthur. <u>The Analects of Confucius</u>. New York: Vintage Books, 1938.

Wallace, Anthony F. "Revitalization Movements," <u>American Anthropologist</u>, Vol. 58, April, 1956, pp. 264-281.

Wallace, Anthony F. C. <u>Religion: An Anthropological View</u>. New York: Random House, 1966.

Ward, Martha C., and Zachary Gussow. "Coping and Adaptation: Community Response and the New Orleans Vietnamese." Paper presented at the Conference on Indochinese Refugees. Fairfax, Virginia: George Mason University, October 24-25, 1979.

Ward, Martha, and Zachary Gussow. "The Vietnamese in New Orleans: A Preliminary Report," <u>Perspective on Ethnicity in New Orleans</u>. New Orleans: University of New Orleans Press, 1979.

Webb, Kate. <u>On the Other Side, 23 Days with the Viet Cong</u>. New York: Quadrangle Books, 1972.

Weher, Max. <u>The Protestant Ethic and the Spirit of Capitalism</u>. New York: Charles Scribneis Son, 1958.

Weinstock, Klaus. "Motivation and Social Structure in the Study of Acculturation," <u>Human Organization</u>, Vol. 52, Spring, 1964, p. 51.

Weiss, Martin G. "Dyads and Groups: A Quantitative Study of Social Ties Among Japanese Immigrants in Brazil," <u>Papers in Anthropology</u>, Vol. 16, No. 1, Spring, 1975, pp. 58-71.

Wenk, Michael G. "Adjustment and Assimilation: The Cuban Experience," <u>International Migration Review</u>, Vol. 3, No. 1, 1968, pp. 38-49.

White, Peper A.   "The Lands and Peoples of Southeast Asia," National Geographic, Vol. 139, No. 3, March, 1971, pp. 296-365.

Whitecotton, Joseph W.   "Tradition and Modernity in Northern New Mexico: An Introduction," Papers in Anthropology, Vol. 17, No. 2, Fall, 1976.

Whitefield, Danny J.   Historical and Cultural Dictionary of Vietnam. Metuchen, N.J.: Scarecrow Press, 1976.

Whitmore, John K., ed.   An Introduction to Indochinese History, Culture, Language and Life--for Persons Involved with the Indochinese Education and Resettlement Project in the State of Michigan. Ann Arbor: University of Michigan, Center for South and Southeast Asian Studies, 1979.

William, Lea E.   Southeast Asia: A History.   New York: Oxford University Press, 1976.

Woolenberg, Charles, ed.   Ethnic Conflict in California History. Tinnon-Brown, Inc. Publishers, 1970.

Wong, Janlee.   "Indochinese Refugee: the Mental Health Perspective," Civil Rights Issues of Asian and Pacific Americans: Myths and Realities. A consultation sponsored by the United States Commission on Civil Rights. Washington, D.C., May 8-9, 1979.

Wong, Morrison G., and Charles Hirschman.   "The New Asian Immigrants," Comparative Studies of Immigration and Ethnicity. Durham, N.C.: Duke University, Center for International Studies, 1979.

Woods, Clyde M.   Culture Change. Dubuque, Iowa: Wm. C. Brown, 1975.

Yamamoto, Joe and others.   "Chinese-Speaking Vietnamese Refugees in Los Angeles: A Preliminary Investigation," Current Perspectives in Cultural Psychiatry. Edited by Edward F. Foulks, Ronald Wintrob, Joseph Westermeyer, and Armando R. Favazza.   New York: Spectrum Publications, Inc., 1976.

Yinger, J. Milton. _Toward a Theory of Assimilation_. Presented at World .Congress of Sociology, Uppsala, Sweden, August, 1978.

Zollschan, George K., and Walter Hirsch, ed. _Social Change: Explorations, Diagnoses and Conjectures_. New York: John Wiley and Sons, 1976.

APPENDIX I

DIRECTORY OF REFUGEE ORGANIZATIONS

International

Intergovernmental Committee for Migration (ICM): P.O. Box 100 CH-1211 Geneva 19, Switzerland. Director: James Carlin. Regional representative: Richard Scott, Suite 2122, 60 E. 42nd St., New York, NY 10165. Tele: 212/599-0440.

International Committee of the Red Cross (ICRC): 17, avenue de la Paix, CH-1211 Geneva, Switzerland.

International Council of Voluntary Agencies (ICVA): 17, avenue de la Paix, 1202 Geneva, Switzerland. Tel.: 33 20 25. Executive Director: Anthony Kozlowski.

International Disaster Institute: 85 Marylebone High St., London WIM 3DE. Director: Dr. Frances D'Souza.

Office of the United Nations High Commissioner for Refugees (UNHCR): Palais des Nations, 1211 Geneva 10, Switzerland. High Commissioner: Poul Harling. Regional office: UN Bldg., 3rd fl., New York, NY 10017. Tel.: 212-754-7600. Washington Liaison Office: UNHCR, 1785 Massachusetts Ave., NW, Washington, DC 20036. Tele.: 202/387-8546. (Liaison with U.S.)

U.S. Goverment

Department of Health and Human Services, Office of Refugee Resettlement: 230 C St., SW, Room 1229, Washington, DC 20201. Tel.: 202/245-0418

Office of the United States Coordinator for Refugee Affairs: Room 7626, Department of State, Washington, DC 20520. Tel.: 202/632-3964. Refugee Program Office, Room 6313, Department of State, WAshington, DC 20520. Tel.: 202/632-5833.

Senate Judiciary Committee: 132 Russell Senate Office Building, Washington, DC 20510. Tele.: 202/224-8050. Strom Thurmond, Chairman. Subcommittee on Immigration and Refugee Policy: Alan Simpson, Chairman.

Selected U.S. Voluntary Agencies

American Bar Association Indochinese Refugee Legal Assistance Program: 800/334-0074. (In North Carolina, call 919/684-6418, not toll-free).

American Friends Service Committee: 1501 Cherry St., Philadelphia, PA 19102. Tel.: 215-241-7000. Executive Secretary: Asia Bennett.

American National Red Cross: 17th and D Streets, NW, Washington, DC 20006. Tel.: 202/737-8300.

American Refugee Committee: 310 Fourth Ave. South, Room 410, Minneapolis, MN 55415. Tele.: 612/332-5365. National Director: Stanley B. Breen.

(R) Buddhist Council for Refugee Rescue and Resettlement: City of 10,000 Buddhas, Box 217, Talmage, CA 95481. Tel.: 707/468-9155. Executive Co-Director: David Rounds.

Catholic Relief Services - U.S.C.C. (CRS): 1011 First Ave., New York, NY 10022. Tele.: 212/838-4700. Executive Director: Most Rev. Edwin B. Broderick, D.D.

(R) Church World Service: 475 Riverside Dr., New York, NY 10115. Immigration and Refugee Program. Tele.: 212/870-2164. Executive Director: Paul F. McCleary.

International Christian Aid: 800 Colorado Blvd., Los Angeles, CA 90041. Tel.: 213/254-4371. President: Joe Bass.

Indochina Refugee Action Center (IRAC): 1025 15th St., NW - Suite 700, Washington, DC 20005. Tel.: 202/347-8903. Director Jesse Bunch.

(R) Lutheran Immigration and Refugee Service/Lutheran
    Council in the U.S.A.: 360 Park Avenue South,
    New York, NY 10010. Tel.: 212/532-6450.
    Director: Ingrid Walter.

Migration and Refugee Services (M.R.S.): United
    States Catholic Conference: 1312 Massachusetts
    Avenue, NW, Washington, DC 20005. Tel.:
    202/659-6618. Executive Director: John
    McCarthy.

(R) World Relief Refugee Services: National Associ-
    ation of Evangelicals, P. O. Box WRC, Nyack, NY
    10960. Tel.: 914/353-1444. Vice-President,
    T. G. Mangham.

APPENDIX II

REFUGEE BIBLIOGRAPHIES

A Bibliography on Refugees. "UNHCR" (a publication), No. 4 (Oct.-Nov. 1980). UNHCR, UN Bldg., 3rd floor, New York, NY 10017.

The Resettlement of Indochinese Refugees in the United States: A Selected Bibliography. Indochina Refugee Action Center, 1025 15th St., NW, Suite 600, Washington, D.C. 20005. Sept. 1980.

Selected Bibliography: Refugees and Refugee Migration. Church World Service, 475 Riverside Dr., Rm. 666, New York, NY 10027. Oct. 1980.

English Language Resource Center: Center for Applied Linguistics, 3520 Prospect St., NW, Washington, D.C. 20007. Rel.: 800/424-3750. Local residents call 202/298-9292.

Indochinese Materials Center: U.S. Department of Education, 324 E. 11th St., 9th Floor, Kansas City, MO 64106.

REFUGEE REPORTS

Office of the U.S. Coordinator for Refugee Affairs. Overview of World Refugee Situation, Aug. 1980. Department of State, Washington, D.C. 20520.

Refugee Reports. American Public Welfare Association 1125 15th St., NW, Suite 300, Washington, D.C. 20005. Published biweekly.

Selected Commission on Immigration and Refugee Policy. U.S. Immigration Policy and the National Interests, Feb. 1981. Select Commission, 726 Jackson Place, New Executive Office Bldg., Rm. 2020, Washington, D.C. 20506.

U.S. Senate, Committee on the Judiciary, and U.S. House of Representative, Committee on the Judiciary, each have published a number of reports on specific legislation or about the refugee situation in a particular geographic area. Address: Senate Judiciary Committee, 2304 Dirksen Senate Office Bldg., Washington, D.C. 20510; House Judiciary Committee, B370B Rayburn House Office Bldg., Washington, D.C. 20515.

APPENDIX IV
INDOCHINESE REFUGEE CAMP POPULATIONS

Boat Camps	Population End of 1979	1980 Arrivals	1980 Departures	Population End of 1980
Australia	149	--	22	127
Brunei	16	29	16	29
China	70	220	150	240
Hong Kong	55,078	14,000	36,000	33,078
Indonesia	32,406	7,200	35,600	4,006
Japan	1,243	1,050	640	1,664
Korea	166	--	97	69
Macau	3,408	2,300	3,050	2,658
Malyasia	34,927	20,000	41,500	13,427
Philippines	4,315	5,500	6,400	3,415
Singapore	886	10,000	8,200	2,686
Thailand	6,789	21,000	21,000	6,789
Other Countires	67	1	38	30
Boat Camps Subtotal	139,531	81,299	152,713	68,118
Land Camps*				
Thailand	141,191	45,000	106,000	80,191
Total	280,722	126,300	258,713	148,309

*Figures do not include Kampucheans fleeing Heng Samrin/Vietnamese invasion. This total estimated to be 150,000 in camps within Kampuchea along in Thai border.

Source: 1981 World Refugee Survey. A publication of the United States Committee for Refugee.

118

APPENDIX V

INDOCHINA REFUGEE RESETTLEMENT BY COUNTRY

Country	1979 est. Population (Millions)	Total Refugees Through 8/30/80	Refugees Per# Inhabitants
U.S.	220.3	389,000	1 to 566
Peoples Republic of China	950.0	240,000	1 to 3,958
France	53.4	76,288	1 to 700
Canada	23.7	52,348	1 to 453
Australia	14.4	37,756	1 to 380
F.R. Germany	61.2	14,013	1 to 4,371
United Kingdom	55.8	13,087	1 to 4,292
Malaysia	13.3	2,191	1 to 4,586
Switzerland	6.3	3,273	1 to 1,969
Belgium	9.8	3,447	1 to 2,882
Norway	4.1	3,289	1 to 1,242
Sweden	8.3	2,267	1 to 3,608
Argentina	26.7	4,500	1 to 5,933
Taiwan	17.3	1,000	1 to 17,300
Denmark	5.1	1,370	1 to 3,642
Italy	56.9	1,365	1 to 41,684
Netherlands	14.0	1,980	1 to 7,071
Spain	37.6	1,001	1 to 37,600
Zimbabwe-Rhodesia	7.2	1,000	1 to 7,200

Information provided by the Indochina Refugee Action
Center, Washington, D.C.

APPENDIX VI

VOLUTEER AGENCY ASSISTANCE OCTOBER 1978 TO JANUARY 1981

Voluntary Agency	Number Resettled
ACNS (American Council for Nationalities Services	35,216
AFCR (American Fund for Czechoslovak Refugees)	6,771
BC (Buddhist Council for Refugee Rescue and Resettlement	85
CWS (Church World Service)	33,978
HIAS (Hebrew Immigrant Aid Society)	9,265
IRC (International Rescue Committee) . . .	26,737
IDHO (State of Idaho Program)	21
IRSC (Iowa Refugee Service Center)	2,071
LIRS (Lutheran Immigration and Refugee Service)	24,359
TF (Tolstoy Foundation)	4,799
USCC (United States Catholic Conference). .	113,974
WRRS (World Relief Refugee Services). . . .	11,437
YMCA (Young Men's Christian Association). .	2,313
TOTAL	271,026

Resettlement of Indochinese refugees in the United States, listed by the number of people assisted by each of 11 voluntary agencies and 2 states, in the 27-month period October 1, 1978, to January 1, 1981.

Source: United States Committee for Refugees.

APPENDIX VII

BASIC VIETNAMESE CUSTOMS

1. The family is the basis of society, not the individual.

2. Three to four generations may reside together in one home.

3. Within the family, the wife deals with all household matters. The husband deals with the outside world (the family is partiarchical).

4. The elderly (parents) are supported by married or unmarried children until they die.

5. Names are written as follows: Family name, Middle name, Given name, e.g., Nguyen Van Hai. The family name is placed first as an emphasis on the person's heritage.

6. Family members use different given names.

7. A large family is traditional.

8. Children reside with their parents until marriage. The males marry between the age of 20 and 30, while the females marry between the ages of 18 and 25.

9. The marriages must be approved by the parents of both the male and female. This is true regardless of ages. (Not a legal requirement, but a traditional one.)

10. First cousins and their children cannot marry each other up to three generations.

11. The celebration of marriage is preferred in the home of one of the marriage participants, not in a church or temple.

12. Legally, women keep their own names after marriage. Formally, married women use their husband's name.

   Example
   Husband's name   Nguyen Van Hai
   Wife's maiden name   Le Thi Ba

Wife's married name		Le Thi Ba
Wife's formal name	.	Mrs. Nguyen Van Hai

13. After marriage, the wife lives with her husband's family. She is considered to "belong" to her husband's family.

14. Before 1959, Vietnamese men could have multiple wives (polygyny). Ranking developed according to responsibility among the wives. Following entrance into the U.S., only one spouse remains married to the husband and second or subsequent marriages may be dissolved. Wives are still informally accepted as family in U.S.

15. When a child is born, they are considered one year old.

16. Sons are more highly valued than daughters.

17. The eldest son has a duty to perform the ancestor worship at home.

18. Brothers and sisters do not touch or kiss one another.

19. If a parent dies, the children customarily wait three years before marrying.

20. If a wife dies, the husband must wait one year before remarrying.

21. If a sibling dies, the others must wait one year to marry.

22. To show respect, Vietnamese will bow their heads in front of a superior or aged person.

23. While conversing, one should not look steadily at a respected person's eyes.

24. Women do not shake hands with each other or with men.

25. Women do not smoke in public.

26. Vietnamese never touch another's head. Only the elderly can touch the heads of young children.

27. Summoning a person with a hand or finger in an up position is reserved only for animals or inferior persons. Between two equal people, it is a provocation. To summon an individual, the entire hand with fingers facing downward is the only appropriate hand signal.

28. Persons of the same sex may hold hands in public and/or sleep in the same bed without public derision.

29. Incest is punished by law and strongly resented by society.

30. The concept of equality between the sexes is the same as in Western countries, but man is still considered slightly superior to woman, socially.

31. The symbol of nationhood (Vietnamese) is the yellow dragon. Yellow is the color of royalty. The dragon symbolizes descent of the Vietnamese from the mythical dragon.

Source: Compiled from interviews with various Vietnamese persons residing in Oklahoma City and from Vuong G. Thuy, Getting to Know the Vietnamese and Their Culture.

APPENDIX VIII

SAMPLE QUESTIONS INITIALLY EMPLOYED OF VIETNAMESE PERSONS IN OKLAHOMA CITY VIETNAMESE STUDY

1. What is your name?

2. How long have you been in the United States?

3. How long have you been in Oklahoma?

4. Are you happy to be here?

5. Did you spend any time in a refugee camp?

6. How many of your family are here?

7. Are any of your family still in Vietnam?

8. Why did you choose to live in Oklahoma City?

9. Do you plan to stay in Oklahoma City?

10. Do you have a job?

11. Have you studied English here?

12. Do you ever go to the Vietnamese American Association?

13. Do you have a certain religion?

14. Do you go to meetings with your religious group?

15. Do you have friends in the other religious groups?

16. What is more important to you? Being _____ (Buddhist, Catholic, etc.) or being Vietnamese?

17. Does the Vietnamese American Association play a role in your religion?

18. Do you plan to stay in America?

19. Is your religion here any different than the way it was in Vietnam?

20. Would you object to my visiting your church (temple, etc.) and talking with your priest (monk, etc.)?

APPENDIX IX

SAMPLE QUESTIONS INITIALLY EMPLOYED OF NON-VIETNAMESE RELIGIOUS LEADERS IN VIETNAMESE STUDY

1. Do you work with the Vietnamese in Oklahoma City?

2. How many Vietnamese are in the city?

3. Are many of the Vietnamese seeking assistance from the local Christian churches or local Christian agencies?

4. Have any of the Vietnamese people joined any of your denomination's churches?

5. Do you understand the reason for Christian church attendance to be that of economic need or religious conversion?

6. To what extent does your group provide economic or material assistance to the Vietnamese refugees?

7. How would you characterize the Vietnamese community in OKC?

8. Are the Vietnamese making cultural adjustments or is that necessary?

9. What do you understand to be the basic cultural characteristics of the Vietnamese religions?

10. What are the Vietnamese religions?

11. How strong are the Vietnamese Buddhists?

12. How strong are the Vietnamese Catholics?

13. Are any of the Buddhists or Catholics joining other churches? If so, why?

14. Where do the Vietnamese Buddhist meet to worship?

15. What patterns, if any, do you see emerging from the first few years of Vietnamese settlement in OKC?

16. What role do the Baptist have with the Vietnamese community? (If the person being asked was Baptist then the question was asked of Catholics. If Catholic, the Baptists or Lutherans, etc.)

17. How do you identify ethnicity with the Vietnamese people?

18. Are religion and ethnicity related in any way?

19. Do you know of any persons practicing Cao Dai in Oklahoma City?

20. What is the relationship between the Oklahoma City Catholic Vietnamese and the Oklahoma City Buddhist Vietnamese?

21. What do you think the future is for the Oklahoma City Vietnamese?

22. Do you think some will return to Vietnam or do you think they would ever desire to return?

SAMPLE QUESTIONS INITIALLY EMPLOYED OF NON-VIETNAMESE
RESIDENTS LIVING WITHIN THE AREA OF
THE BUDDHIST TEMPLE

1. What is your name?

2. How long have you lived in this neighborhood?

3. Are there any Vietnamese people living in this area?

4. Is there a Buddhist Church close by?

5. Have you ever been there?

6. Have you ever met any of the Vietnamese Buddhists?

7. What do you think of the Vietnamese Buddhists?

8. Can you tell me something about what the Buddhist believe?

9. Do you have a religion?

10. What is the difference between your religion and Buddhism?

11. How do you feel about having the Buddhist church in your neighborhood?

12. Anything else you can tell me?

APPENDIX XI

SAMPLE OF COMMUNITY PROGRAM SPONSORED BY THE
VIETNAMESE AMERICAN ASSOCIATION

VIETNAMESE AMERICAN ASSOCIATION
Workshop #1 (English)
Indochinese Refugees Resettlement
In Oklahoma
"The New Experience"
Friday, October 3rd, 1980
at the Sheraton Century Center
Downtown Oklahoma City

9:00   Registration

9:30   Welcome

Topics	Speakers
-VAA's mental health project: Experience and achievements	-Dao The Xuong
-Federal Government Programs for Refugees	-Carol Sedanko
-Refugee Resettlement in the State of Oklahoma	-John E. Searle

10:30 Coffee Break

-Role of the bilingual education in refugee resettlement process	-Vuong Gia Thuy
-The increasing involvement of Mutual Assistance Associations in the resettlement of refugees	-Nguyen Dinh Thu
-The influence of the Vietnamese culture in refugee adjustment	-Vuong Gia Thuy

12:30 Lunch

1:30   Panel discussion and   -Carol Sedanko
       questions   John E. Searle
                                    Nguyen Dihn Thu
                                    Dao The Xuong

3:00   Closing remarks